# Merlin R. Carothers

# Bringing Heaven Into Hell

*edited by*
Jorunn Oftedal Ricketts

MERLIN R. CAROTHERS COMPANY
ESCONDIDO, CALIFORNIA

ISBN: 0-943026-10-5

Unless otherwise identified, all scriptures are from the
Living Bible translated by Ken Taylor Paraphrased
(Wheaton, IL Tyndale House, Publishers, © 1971). Used
by special permission.

# CONTENTS

*Unless otherwise noted, all Scripture references are taken from the paraphrased Living Bible.*

**Merlin R. Carothers**
*best-selling author of*

PRISON TO PRAISE
POWER IN PRAISE
ANSWERS TO PRAISE
PRAISE WORKS
WALKING AND LEAPING
VICTORY ON PRAISE MOUNTAIN
MORE POWER TO YOU
THE BIBLE ON PRAISE
PRISON TO PRAISE — Large Print
*Over 8,000,000 copies combined*
*Praise Books by Merlin Carothers now printed in 32 foreign languages.*

# 1. What Is Praise?

For seven exciting years, I have written and taught about Praise, yet I am beginning to see that so far I am barely into the kindergarten of Praise myself. This is no statement of false humility. Each day I am more convinced that I know very little of all there is to learn about praising God. In fact, I am finding out that praising Him is one of the most important things I can learn while I am here on earth — because to praise Him, as he intends for us to praise, involves every aspect of my life.

Praise is meant to be the focal point of our relationship with God.

Over the years I have seen thousands of people approach the subject of praising God. For some, praise revolutionized their lives. For others, it meant nothing. I have observed the same contrast in my own life. Sometimes praise "works". Sometimes my words of praise fall flat and empty.

What makes the difference?

First of all: praise can never be a surface thing. It isn't saying, "Praise the Lord, Praise the Lord," all day long. The secret is something that flows from the center of what is really you. It is something that brings an immediate response from the heart of God.

This something is "true Praise." What does it consist of? What conditions must be present in our lives for our praise to be true? What conditions in our lives hinder praise? If I live to be a hundred years old, I expect to be still learning more about the answers.

Beyond the mechanics of praise lies the heart of praise and the way actually to bring Heaven into Hell. More than anything else in this world, I want to understand more of how God wants me to praise Him. More than anything else, I want my heart to flow in a continuous stream of worship to God.

Suffering draws people together. If you suffer, and think others do not, you will be convinced they could not possibly understand you. If you read my books and think, "Merlin doesn't really have to suffer because God always answers his prayers immediately," you wouldn't believe I could help you. But I do suffer, and God often permits me to wait a long while before He shows me the results of trusting Him. I was once charged with misappropriating church funds, and by someone I had loved and trusted. There was absolutely no basis for the charge and no evidence of even the slightest kind. A judge looked at the charge for a few minutes and responded with, "What is this doing here? There isn't any evidence of even a mistake in judgment by this defendant." But the vicious harm had been done. My reputation had been attacked, and this was all the accuser wanted to do. Many people would leap at the opportunity to declare, "I knew something was wrong all the time" or "Here is proof that praise pays — in dollars." On and on the accusations could go. But the point is — I want to learn obedience even as He learned it. "Though he were a Son, yet learned he obedience by the things which he suffered." (Heb. 5:8 KJV)

I pray that as I share with you some of the things I am learning, you, too, will want to stretch and grow and open your heart to the flow of praise that glorifies God and demonstrates His love and power.

## 2. From "Big-Shot" To Nothing . . .

The solid steel door clanged shut, and the prisoner was alone in the tiny underground cell. The words of the guard still rang in his ears, "Get in there, big-shot — we'll be back for you in fifty years!"

It was no nightmare. On the "outside" the prisoner had been a well-known criminal lawyer, enjoying the power and luxuries that money and the right connections could supply. He had lived what he believed: "If you like it — do it. If you want it — get it."

It was the liking for excitement that led him into big-time crime: smuggling dope, dealing in guns and explosives, bank robberies, and insurance frauds. His connections were big names in organized crime. At forty, when his power was rising fast, he was caught selling drugs. All was lost. His wife and two small children were left desolate. He faced a first sentence of fifty years with more charges pending. They would be added on if he lived long enough to be even considered for parole.

The walls of the cell were smeared with blood and human excrement. Some poor prisoner before him had kept track of the years with pencil marks on the concrete: ten years — twenty years — thirty years. There was no escape. The cell was dark and damp, and the silence only broken by the clanging of steel doors down the corridor and the screams of a prisoner pushed to the brink of insanity.

Stripped of the glamor and success of the outside world, suddenly completely helpless, the prisoner felt as if he were buried alive in a stinking grave, forgotten and alone. Overcome, he fell to his knees on the cold floor. Like a child he sobbed, "Oh, God — I don't even know if You exist, but if You're out there and can hear me — I am so very, very sorry for what I have done. Please forgive me. If you will only forgive me and give me one last chance, I'll give You my whole life — everything — every bit of me. Forever!"

The darkness remained silent, but something had happened. The fear and horror were gone. Instead he was filled with an overwhelming sense of being forgiven and loved. Warm tears of gratitude rolled down the prisoner's face. He felt like a small boy who comes to his father to ask forgiveness and is caught up in loving, strong arms.

The loathsome cell was no longer a place of loneliness and despair. Gone was even the desire to get away from there. "Never had I felt so free — so happy," the prisoner wrote me. "I thanked God from the bottom of my heart for bringing me into that stinking little hole to meet him."

The prisoner was Dr. Gene Neill. I first learned of his existence when he wrote to tell me he had received the book, *Power in Praise.* After surrendering his life to God, he eagerly studied the Bible someone had smuggled into his cell. More than anything he wanted to know God's instructions for his life. Reading *Power in Praise,* it became even clearer that God wanted him to be thankful in every circumstance.

So he thanked God for the lice and the cockroaches and for the abuses of the guards. He gave thanks for the stench of urine and filth. He praised God for his five-year-old son who would be a middle-aged man before his father was released from prison. He even praised God for the greed and callousness of his own heart that had driven him to destroy his family.

Praising God brought remarkable results in Gene Neill's life. Aside from his being filled with joy, others were affected, too. Fellow prisoners and guards turned their lives over to God.

Before long, Gene was transferred from the high-security prison to a prison-camp in the Florida swamps. Nearly eaten up by mosquitoes, he thanked God for the insects — and they stopped biting him. His fellow prisoners were certain he had smuggled in some high-powered bug-spray. Soon the other men began to respond to the power of God they saw demonstrated in Gene's life.

After two years, Gene was released from prison. A full pardon was issued from Washington, D.C. He was free to join his wife and family, who now lived nearby in poverty. Together they thanked God for their circumstances, and through a series of happenings, their daily needs were met. Once a stranger stopped them on the street to give Gene a sum of money without any other explanation than: "God told me to give you this!" Another time they were giving thanks for their meagre diet when someone knocked on the door of the old, converted bus the Neills called "home." He handed them a package of T-bone steaks and left.

Why did praise "work" in Gene Neill's case? What was that something that flowed from his heart and met with such immediate response from God?

The key is found in one word: forgiveness.

Gene asked to be forgiven — and surrendered his life into God's hands. God's response was instant. It always is.

True praise is the natural response from a heart that has been forgiven. Forgiveness is a necessary foundation for praise — it holds the key to our entire relationship with God.

No one knows our nature better than God who made us. He knows we are disobedient, and that our disobedience separates us from Him. He longs for a restoration of our broken relationship, and since He knows He can't depend on us to do anything right, He decided a long time ago to depend on Himself instead. Our disobedience deserves death, so God let His own Son, Jesus Christ, die for us. Thus our debt is paid and God's system of forgiveness has been set up.

"Forgiveness" means to give up the claim to compensation from an offender. We are the offenders. Based on what Jesus has done, God gives up all claims to repayment from us. He holds nothing against us. It sounds so simple, but it is obvious that we don't understand it fully. If we did, we would be overwhelmed with gratitude and filled with joy for the rest of our lives. Most of us undervalue God's system of forgiveness. We can only be thankful that He doesn't!

The plan of redemption is designed to restore our relation with God, but it doesn't work unless we accept it. You would think that the idea of being set free from all guilt would thrill us — instead, we balk — because our part in the system involves admitting that we are wrong. I think the hardest thing we human beings do is to admit that we can't do anything right. We do almost anything to keep from swallowing our pride and accepting what God has done for us.

Part of the reason is that we have been taught from childhood to "do our own share" — earn our own way. We are proud to be "self-made," and to say, "Look at Joe, look at Susie — they've made something of themselves in this world."

Pride in our own accomplishments separates us from God. We want to handle things on our own, and we struggle along until our problems and pain become unbearable. Even then, we try to resist God's solution and say, "I'd be ashamed to come to God like a beggar. I'll wait till I get myself out of this mess first!"

Some of us try a half-hearted confession. We *say* we are sorry, but our actions deny our words, and we go right back to doing what we did before. A vital ingredient is lacking in our repentance — the element of surrender to God's will. Surrender means to give up oneself into the power of another. To do anything less in our relationship with God is only to kid ourselves. It probably means we aren't really sorry for doing wrong, but only for getting caught.

The true forgiveness that restores our relationship with God hinges on our surrender to His will. Without it we will be like a runaway child who decides to come home when things get rough out in the world. He may say, "I'm sorry I ran away, and I want to come home. But I don't like your rules — I want to be independent, and I'm going to wear my hair and my clothes the way I like and do what I want."

Have you treated God like that? Do you say, "God, I'm hurting now, and if you'll get me out of this mess, I'll try not to do it again"? If you are not really sincere, God reads your secret thoughts: "But I like doing what I'm doing, and I'll keep on with it as long as I get away with it . . ."

We won't be able to have a close relationship with God that way, any more than a restless runaway will be content to stay with Mom and Dad for very long.

In contrast, the Bible tells a story about a father-son relationship that was completely restored. The son took his inheritance and left home. He lived in luxury in a far-off country until his money ran out and his friends left him. Hungry and alone, he begged a farmer for work and was allowed to feed the pigs. He ate what the pigs left and slept with them. It was not a very pleasant way of life, and one day the boy came to his senses and realized he had done wrong. In his father's house, even the servants lived in comfort and had plenty to eat.

Deeply regretting his mistake, he knew that he had spent his inheritance and no longer had a right to be treated like a son. But he decided to ask his father for a job on the farm. He was willing to do the most menial labor. With that in mind, he hurried home, and when his father came to meet him, he cried out, "I have sinned against heaven and you, and I am not worthy of being called your son!"

Instead of scolding him, the father was overjoyed. He embraced him, dressed him in new clothes, and placed rings on his fingers to signify that he was a rightful heir and son. Then he gave orders to kill a fatted calf for a big homecoming celebration. (Luke 15)

In the same way, God waits for each of us to return from our land of disobedience. When we admit that we have done wrong and are ready to let God order our lives, His response is like the father's in the story. He rejoices that we have come home, clothes us in new robes, and calls for a great celebration, because "my child who was lost has been found."

The Father's forgiveness is waiting — but some of us won't return home to accept it. What if the prodigal son had been sorry for his wrong-doing, but never came home to ask his father's forgiveness? There are some very unhappy people who bitterly regret the condition their lives have fallen into, and who cry with remorse for their guilt, but who will not ask God's forgiveness.

Judas was like that. He regretted his betrayal of Jesus and tried to pay back the thirty pieces of silver he had received for his act of treason. When that didn't work, his guilt drove him to hang himself. He never heard the words of Jesus on the cross: "Father, forgive them; for they know not what they do . . ." (Luke 23:34 KJV)

Are you so burdened by guilt that you try to destroy yourself? Psychiatrists say that unresolved guilt causes a self-destructive urge. We try to punish ourselves by becoming alcoholics, over-eaters, drug-users, or criminals.

We may think we are too undeserving to be forgiven, and our sins too terrible for God to accept us. Some of us may not understand that God *wants* to forgive us, but more often it is pride that makes us unwilling to accept God's full pardon. We want to take the responsibility for repayment on ourselves, and refuse to admit that God's forgiveness is the only remedy for our guilt.

There are some of us who take only the first step. We admit our faults to God and ask Him to forgive us, but somehow we are unable to believe that *He does*. Over and over again we say that we are sorry, never believing He heard us. Can you imagine the prodigal son in the story coming to his father: "Oh, Dad, I have sinned, please forgive me." Without waiting for a

reply, he repeats, "Oh, Dad, I have sinned, please forgive me."
Every day he cries it, over and over again, never accepting that
his father forgave him the first time.

A prisoner wrote me who had spent most of his life behind
bars. He had been to five reform schools, eleven prisons and
countless jails. On the outside he could never be good enough to
stay out of trouble, and he was convinced that God was
punishing him for being bad by putting him in prison again
and again. Finally, he reached the conclusion that the only
way to get out and stay out was to make himself good enough to
earn God's favor. So he began to read a Bible ten to twelve
hours a day in his cell. "A thousand times a day I asked God to
forgive me, and just as many times I tried to fight off the devil,"
he wrote me. "I thought God was a wrathful judge, and I was
sure He didn't love a sinner like me."

Someone gave him the book, *Power in Praise,* but he
thought the writer was a nut for suggesting he should thank
God for putting him in prison. He continued the struggle to
make himself worthy of God's forgiveness until, finally, one
day he was too exhausted to keep fighting. Sobbing helplessly,
he admitted his failure, "Lord, You'll have to forgive me,
because I'm all fought out. If You want me like I am, come get
me, God, and do what You like with me. But please don't hold it
against me that I can't try to please You any more."

His pillow was wet with tears, but that night he slept like a
baby. "The Lord and I are good friends now," his letter
continued. "He's the best cell partner a guy can ask for. The
words, 'Praise the Lord' even come to me in my sleep. Jesus is
all right. He does love me. He is so real and such a friend when
we give Him credit for what He did for us on the cross."

When we want to pay for our own sin, we refuse to give
Jesus the credit for what He has done. We want God's forgiveness on our terms. Our guilt is an unnecessary burden, carried
only because we are too prideful, too self-willed to lay it down
in God's waiting hands. God's father heart yearns for us. He
says, "My child, I know what you have done. I know every ugly

act, every evil thought. You have sinned against me and others, but I forgive you. Come home. Let me clothe you and feed you and shower you with blessings. Let me love you and heal your wounds and your broken heart."

Our rejection of His forgiveness may not be so obvious. We may say we admit our wrongs and accept His forgiveness, but behave as if we are paying the penalty for our own sins. Many people in that category become Christian workers. They give their lives in service to God as pastors, Sunday school teachers, lay leaders, nuns, or priests, but they labor more out of a sense of duty than of love, and know little joy in serving Christ. All of us, at one time or another, behave like that.

Try to imagine the prodigal son coming home to his father saying, "Dad, I know you forgive me, but I don't deserve a homecoming party. You'll have to celebrate without me. I'm unworthy of living in your house and eating at your table, so I'll stay out in the barn. I promise to slave from sunrise to sunset to make up for the inheritance I wasted. I have no right to be happy ever again. You'll be proud of me, Dad, for the way I pay you back for the horrible thing I did."

Does that sound pious and self-sacrificing in your ears? How do you think it sounds to God when He's already made other arrangements to take care of our guilt?

We may look 'good' in the eyes of others as we play the martyr's role, paying God what we feel we 'owe' Him. But that isn't what *He wants* from us. We are refusing to give Christ credit for canceling our debts. We are rejecting Him as our Savior, and it is pride, not humility, that motivates us.

David addressed himself to God, saying, "You don't want a sacrifice; if You did, how gladly I would do it! You aren't interested in offerings burned before you on the altar. It is a broken spirit You want — remorse and penitence. A broken and a contrite heart, O God, You will not ignore." (Ps. 51:16,17)

It is a proud and unbroken heart that insists on paying for its own sins. Jesus said, "Come unto me, all ye that labour and are heavy laden, and I will give you rest." (Matt. 11:28 KJV)

There is no heavier burden in this world than trying to carry the penalty for our own sins. As long as we do, we will never know God's forgiveness. We will never know the joy of a cleansed heart. Our relationship with God can never be a close one. Our praise can never become more than empty words.

What a tremendous load rolls off our back when we learn to accept God's forgiveness completely. Our need for it should not be a source of despair, but of rejoicing. Only a heart that has been forgiven understands the love of God. The more we are forgiven, the more we love Him, and the more we are able to praise Him. Then we can sing with David, "What happiness for those whose guilt has been forgiven! What joys when sins are covered over! What relief for those who have confessed their sins and God has cleared their record . . . So rejoice in Him, all those who are His, and shout for joy, all those who try to obey Him." (Ps. 32:1,2,11)

## 3. Three-Way Forgiveness

Steve lost his Dad in a two-car accident. A policeman who was an eyewitness reported that the other driver was entirely to blame — and came away without a scratch. Anger and grief settled deep in Steve's heart.

A year later Steve became a Christian, but found no lasting peace. The grief over his father and bitterness against the man who had killed him preyed on his mind day and night. He begged God to take it away, but it only seemed worse.

Someone gave Steve *Prison to Praise*, and he haltingly tried to praise God for the accident that took his father's life. Now suddenly he could see that his grief and hatred were rooted in his unwillingness to forgive the other man. With eyes opened to his own sin, Steve asked forgiveness for his hatred and help to forgive. He wrote me, "It has been several months now, and I am actually growing to love the man who drove the other car. God loves him, and so should I. What a glorious peace I have found."

Praise opened the way to forgiveness in Steve's heart, but had he refused to forgive, his praise would have remained mechanical and brought no fruit. An unforgiving heart cannot be a heart of praise. Forgiveness not only holds the key to our relationship with God, but also to our relationship with others. In fact, God has made one dependent on the other. Forgiveness is a three-way proposition.

Jesus said, "Your heavenly Father will forgive you if you forgive those who sin against you; but if you refuse to forgive them, He will not forgive you." (Matt. 6:14,15)

God forgives us immediately when we confess our sins to Him. That is His nature. But if we don't go on to forgive others, we will suffer. Unforgiveness will rob us of peace, joy, and health. God made us that way. He built it into us, and we have no control over it.

A young woman came to me with a problem that threatened to ruin her marriage. She found it nearly impossible to respond in love to her husband. Instead, she felt resentment and fear at his touch. She loved her husband, and could not understand her own behavior. No matter how hard she tried, she could not change herself.

As she talked, I began to get a picture of an extremely unhappy childhood. Her father had abused and beaten her repeatedly. When she tried to hide under the bed, he pulled her out by the hair to beat her some more. Fear and bitterness had festered in her heart for years, until she felt a repulsion towards all men, including her husband. In addition, she felt guilty for hating her own father, although she had repressed both her hatred and her guilt so that she seldom thought of it any more.

The young lady was able to accept God's forgiveness for her attitude of unforgiveness, and to understand that God forgave her father as well. When she was able to forgive her father, the fear and resentment towards her husband disappeared, and she was free to respond to his love.

Often the root of our present family problems can be found in painful experiences of our childhood. Perhaps a difficult experience with a parent, a sister or brother still haunts us. Old wounds dictate our behavior and until they are healed, we continue to hurt those we most want to love.

One man told how his suspicions and jealousy were about to drive his wife away. As a child he had burned with anger and shame over his mother's promiscuity, and had never been able to forgive her. The unforgiving attitude towards his mother caused him to watch every move his wife made, expecting to discover that she was unfaithful. As soon as he was able to forgive his mother, the suspicions towards his wife faded away.

Without realizing it, we can transpose our feelings from the past to our present relationships. With handicaps like that, no wonder many of us are having difficulties.

Not only are we imprisoned by the unsettled accounts of the past, but so are the people around us. They may react to us because our behavior rubs their old wounds. We need to ask God, "Is there any unforgiveness in me, Lord, that is making me ill or making me unhappy or that is hurting my family?"

We human beings can get ourselves into situations we think are unforgivable, but that simply isn't true. There is no need to repress old memories or keep old wounds covered up, because the Bible declares, "If the Son therefore shall make you free, you shall be free indeed." (John 8:36 KJV). Jesus came to guarantee our forgiveness for everything we've ever done or thought of doing wrong, and to make it possible for us to forgive everything that anyone else has ever done or thought of doing against us. Our sins or the sins of others have no power to bind us when we are forgiven and forgiving.

We can usually think of many reasons why we won't forgive others. "How can I forgive when the people who hurt me don't deserve to be forgiven?" It may be true — they don't deserve it — but we don't deserve to be forgiven either, and God forgives us anyway.

"Never pay back evil for evil . . ." wrote Paul. "Don't let evil get the upper hand but conquer evil by doing good." (Romans 12:17,21) Holding on to unforgiveness is just another way of paying back evil for evil, and by our attitude we give evil the upper hand over us. The only way to conquer evil is to forgive. That is how God overcomes the evil in us. Forgive and God conquers the evil in us by forgiving us. When we forgive and love those who hurt us, evil loses its power over us.

You may get hurt in your physical body if they hit you or torture you — Jesus didn't promise that we would never suffer physically — but they can't upset your peace and joy on the inside. In fact, I guarantee that if you respond to evil with real forgiveness and love, you will experience great joy.

"What happiness it is when others hate you and exclude you and insult you and smear your name because you are mine! When that happens, rejoice! Yes, leap for joy! ..." (Luke 6:22,23) You can only leap for joy when you have forgiven those who hurt you.

Jesus said, "Listen, all of you. Love your *enemies*. Do *good* to those who *hate* you. Pray for the happiness of those who *curse* you; implore God's blessing on those who *hurt* you." (Luke 6:27,28)

To love your enemies you first have to forgive them. If that is difficult, try to think of it this way: God forgives even the worst offenders, and the greater our guilt, the more we have reason to be grateful for his forgiveness. If someone has hurt me; the worse it is, the more he needs to be forgiven, and the greater is my opportunity to be like Christ and to forgive him.

Maybe you don't want that kind of opportunity to practice Christian love, but just think of it; until someone hurts you, you will never know the joy of forgiving!

Sometimes we avoid the issue by saying, "Well, I would forgive that person if only he or she would ask me to forgive." God's forgiveness comes to us even before we ask Him. Jesus, hanging on the cross, said, "Father, forgive them, they don't know what they are doing." The people who mocked Him and beat Him and crucified Him didn't ask His forgiveness, or care if they ever got it. He forgave them anyway, because the Son of God could not do otherwise. And we cannot do otherwise either, if we want to do God's will. He wants us to forgive all those who have ever hurt us in our entire lives, whether or not they know what they did, or want our forgiveness.

Not only does it help us to forgive. God has arranged it so that it also helps those we forgive — even if they are unaware that we've forgiven them. When we ask God, "Forgive them for what they did to me," He does just that. He uses our forgiveness in their lives to begin freeing them from their bondage of guilt and draw them closer to Himself.

Paul was in the crowd watching Stephen being stoned to death. "So they stoned Stephen while he called upon God and said, 'Jesus, Lord, receive my spirit!' Then, on his knees, he cried in ringing tones, 'Lord, forgive them for this sin.' And with these words he fell into the sleep of death, while Saul gave silent assent to his execution." (Acts 7:59,60; 8:1a Phillips) I am sure God was working in Paul's heart that day, and Stephen's words of forgiveness hastened that work.

Our responsibility to forgive others is put to us plainly. Unless we forgive, we keep ourselves and those to whom we refuse forgiveness in bondage, blocking out God's love.

Bill, a prisoner, wrote to tell me how he had experienced God's forgiveness. The very next day in the mess hall, he was confronted with his worst enemy. The two men had tried to kill each other, and for ten years, prison authorities had kept them separated. Their files were stamped with the warning never to put them within reach of each other. But now there had been a slip-up and they were staring at each other across the breakfast table. Bill's first reaction was fear, but then the thought came, "Praise Me for this," and he responded almost automatically, "Thank You, Lord, for letting me face Ron this morning."

Ron was calm as they talked. Bill told about the change Jesus Christ had brought into his life, and the two men parted as friends. In the middle of the night, Bill was awakened with the words ringing in his head, "Forgive Ron!" He said, "Lord, forgive Ron!" and felt peace and a wonderful joy as he went back to sleep. The next morning he received word from Ron that he, too, wanted to meet Jesus.

Forgiveness unlocks our prisons of hatred and ill feeling towards others. Can you imagine what would happen if we all could forgive everyone everything that was ever done to hurt us?

Most of us put a condition on our forgiveness. We say, "Okay, I'll forgive you — if you'll change!" That is not real forgiveness. Forgiveness means to give up any claim to compensation or payment from an offender. That means he doesn't even owe us an apology, and we have no right to expect him to change. To forgive means to accept that person just as he or she is — even if he should continue to do the thing that hurts us over and over and over again.

Peter asked Jesus, "Sir, how often should I forgive a brother who sins against me? Seven times?"

"No!" Jesus replied, "Seventy times seven!" (Matt 18:21,22) If you add that up and say, "Okay — after 490 times I don't have to forgive him any more," you missed the message.

One woman wrote to tell an amazing story of forgiveness. She read the book *Prison to Praise* on the eve of an operation and decided to thank God for the pain she expected to suffer during her recovery. To her great surprise and the surprise of her doctors and nurses, she experienced no pain at all, and did not even need an aspirin for discomfort. Now she was convinced that praising God worked and decided to thank Him for whatever might come into her life from that moment on.

The big test soon came. Her husband announced that he wanted a trial separation. He told her he was contemplating a divorce, but first wanted to see if he could live away from their children. "I realized then that God had allowed me to see the power of praising Him just so I would have the strength to praise Him now," her letter stated.

After a month the husband came home. He could not bear to live apart from his children. However, he also confessed that for the past three years he had loved another woman and desperately wanted to marry her.

"It was agony to watch my husband's pain," the wife wrote. "He was miserable without the woman he loved, yet he could not bear to leave our children. He was in torment, not knowing which way to turn." Still she was determined to praise God for it all. "I began praising Him for the broken marriage vows, for the woman in my husband's life, for the fact that he did not love me and wanted a divorce . . ."

For a year she kept it up. Her husband remained at home all that time, and one day they discovered that they had a new and deeper love for one another than ever before. "It still amazes us both that our love continues to grow, but we have seen that anything is possible with God," she wrote. "He truly turned my mourning into joy and made even such a disaster as ours into something good and beautiful. Praise the Lord!"

The secret of the success in this woman's story does not lie simply in her determination to praise God for it all. The power was released through her praise because she was willing to forgive her husband and accept him just as he was.

Can you imagine how difficult it must have been? The husband did not ask his wife's forgiveness or promise to change. Each day she could see how his thoughts and longings were openly directed towards another woman, yet she was moved with compassion for his agony instead of pity for herself. Most of us would have understood more readily if her reaction had been indignation and bitterness.

I have received letters from other women telling similar stories, but without a happy ending. In those letters the unforgiving spirit was revealed by the bitter and complaining tone, "I have praised God for my situation, but my husband is as intolerable and mean as ever."

A common characteristic of unforgiving people is an un-willingness or perhaps an inability — to see themselves at fault. A lady in our church told me that for years her marriage had been going up and down like a roller-coaster. She and her husband had been divorced once and separated several times. She became a Christian and came to our church because she wanted to learn how to praise God for her husband — in order for God to change him. She thought that her husband's selfishness and demanding attitude caused all their problems.

However, her praise brought no results that she could see. During a three-day separation while she considered divorce again, she promised herself and God that she would make one last try. "I determined to be totally honest with myself and God and not pretend in any way," she told me.

She and her husband came to church the following morn-ing, and during the sermon she became overwhelmed with the feeling that she needed God's forgiveness. Kneeling at the altar she wept and wept, and when she came back to her seat she asked her husband to forgive her as well. "Suddenly my heart just overflowed with gratitude for my husband," she said. "And the strange thing is that all the time I had thought he was at fault. I was angry because he never asked my forgiveness or admitted to being sorry for anything. Now at last I realize I had the whole thing turned upside down. *I* was the selfish and demanding one who needed forgiveness."

Now her praise flowed freely from a heart filled with love and peace. The old restlessness was gone completely.

Jesus told the parable of the servant who owed the king the equivalent of ten million dollars. He could not pay and pleaded for mercy. The king forgave him all his debt, but as soon as the servant was released, he went to a man who owed him the equivalent of two thousand dollars, grabbed him by the throat and demanded instant payment. The man didn't have the money and fell to his knees begging for a little time, but the king's servant refused and had the man thrown in jail until the debt could be paid in full. When the king heard, he called the servant and said, ". . . 'You evil-hearted wretch! Here I forgave you all that tremendous debt, just because you asked me to — shouldn't you have mercy on others, just as I had mercy on you?' Then the angry king sent the man to the torture chamber until he had paid every last penny owed. 'So shall my Heavenly Father do to you, if you refuse to truly forgive your brothers,' " Jesus warns us. (Matt. 18:32-34)

Unforgiveness is a deadly poison — and it is tearing up families every day. Our resentment grows over such little things, and as we hang on to it we don't realize that it masks a dangerous attitude of unforgiveness.

A teenager gets mad because Dad won't let him borrow the family car for the evening. "Why should I forgive him?" he says. "He doesn't trust me!"

Teenager, can you believe that God could change your Dad's mind if He wanted? And if He doesn't, it must be because right now God doesn't want you to take the car. Can you thank God for your Dad? And forgive him? If you do, I guarantee that the atmosphere in your home will be a hundred percent better.

Dad may even let you borrow the family car, but that is not the important point. What you will notice most is that you get rid of that ugly feeling inside that grows every time you think of how rotten and unfair your Dad is.

Sometimes we seem to take pleasure in refusing forgiveness even when we're asked to forgive. Does this scene seem familiar?

A husband complains because he doesn't like TV dinners three days in a row. The wife feels guilty because she neglected to plan her days better. The husband uses ugly words and slams the door as he leaves without eating, but soon he comes back to say, "Honey, I'm sorry I hurt your feelings. Please forgive me."

Here is the opportunity to heal the gap that has come between them, but the wife hides her true feelings behind a "sweet" smile and murmurs, "You didn't hurt me, there's nothing to forgive . . ." Behind her words lurks the resentment and unforgiveness — "You made me feel ashamed. Now I'll let you suffer awhile!"

How many times do we repeat that scene with minor variations when someone hits our sore points? We may use the words, "Sure I forgive you, it was nothing." But our actions make it only too clear that we haven't forgotten the nasty thing he did, and won't let him forget it either.

When someone asks your forgiveness, give it even if you don't think he has hurt you. Your forgiveness means a great deal to him, and is important in his relationship with God.

If we can begin by forgiving the members of our family continuously, what a difference it will make. Instead of being grouchy or irritable or cross with one another, we would say, "Thank you, Lord, that my Dad just broke his word to me for the millionth time. I forgive him, Lord, and please forgive him, too." Or, "Thank You, Lord, that my child forgot to make up his bed again this morning for the umpteenth time. I forgive him." Start reacting like that and the atmosphere in your home and at your dinner table will cause visitors to want to know your secret! Then you can introduce them to Jesus.

What a difference it makes when we start to forgive the difficult people we work with and thank God for them just the way they are.

Roy Wyman became a Christian and read my books on praising God for everything. His corporation was in financial difficulties, and there were ill feelings among the partners. At a board meeting plenty of harsh words were said until it was time for Roy to speak. Always he had been a man of quick temper and angry outbursts. During the entire meeting he had been talking to God under his breath, "Lord, I thank you for these men and for what they are saying. Forgive me my angry feelings, Lord, and I praise you for everything that is happening here." When he opened his mouth to speak, he was surprised at his own words, "All I have left to say to you fellows is that I love you!"

The corporation reorganized when the most difficult partner decided to sell out. Soon the profits began to rise and there were remarkable changes in the personnel, who came to know Christ as their Savior, one by one. Several months later, at a Christian rally in town, the former partner, who had left the corporation in anger, received Christ into his heart. Roy said, "I lost a partner, but, praise God, I soon gained a Christian brother."

Sometimes Christians even have trouble getting along with each other in church! Yet Jesus said, "That's how people will know you are my followers; because you love each other!"

When churches seem cold and Christians harsh and critical of one another, an unforgiving spirit may be quenching all joy and love. If you are in a church like that, start thanking God for putting you there and take a close look at your attitude.

Paul wrote, "Be gentle and ready to forgive; never hold grudges. Remember, the Lord forgave you, so you must forgive others. Most of all, let love guide your life, for then the whole church will stay together in perfect harmony. Let the peace of heart which comes from Christ be always present in your hearts and lives, for this is your responsibility and privilege as members of his Body. And always be thankful." (Col. 3:13,14)

If all Christians had lived up to their responsibility and privilege of loving and forgiving each other, we would have a lot fewer denominations today! It is our wonderful privilege to be forgiving and loving, to let our hearts be filled with peace, and always to be thankful.

If you feel that your spiritual life is at a standstill, then ask God, "What haven't I forgiven?" Do you sometimes think that God Himself has done you wrong? That He hasn't been helping you or hearing your prayers? Then you need to settle it with Him. Tell Him, "God, I don't understand why You have allowed these people to hurt me and these problems to pile up. I have been thinking you weren't concerned about me. You weren't bringing good things into my life. Please forgive me for thinking that way. I want to believe You love me and are working every problem in my life for my good."

My friend, Gene Neill, told me about Roy Roach, who was arrested for something he had not done and put in the same prison with Gene at Eglin Air Force Base Federal Prison at Fort Walton Beach, Florida. The false testimony of another man resulted in Roy's conviction. One day he heard that the other man had been caught for another offense and had landed in the same prison. Hatred and bitterness rose up, and Roy began to plot the murder of his false accuser. He confided in Gene, who suggested that Roy should give up his plans for murder and instead thank God for the whole situation. The idea didn't make any sense to Roy, who continued with his plot to murder.

One day he was told that his wife and daughter had both been diagnosed as having terminal cancer. In agony he pleaded with God to help them, and begged Gene to pray with him. Gene repeated his suggestion that Roy should thank God for everything. Despair had brought Roy to the end of his rope. On his knees he surrendered his hatred for the other man, asked forgiveness and was able to praise God for being in prison and for the illness of his wife and daughter. He was able to believe that God was using all these calamities for His glory and the family's good.

In two weeks an absolutely amazing thing happened. Roy's wife and daughter came with the report that all symptoms of cancer were gone. X-rays showed no trace of illness. Roy's forgiveness released the power of God to heal.

Are you treated unfairly? Suffering innocently? Can you believe God intends it for good? Joseph was sold by his own brothers into slavery in Egypt. Later he spent two years in prison for something he hadn't done. After he had been restored to freedom and put in the highest position in the land, next to Pharaoh, his brothers came to buy grain from him. They were horrified when they recognized him, certain that he would take revenge. But Joseph said, ". . . Ye thought evil against me; but God meant it unto good . . ." (Gen. 50:20 KJV)

It makes no difference that those who hurt you intend to do evil. God won't let any harm come to you unless He means it for good. If you can believe that, can you praise Him for it? Can you be so forgiving that you are actually glad they did it? A glad-glad, happy-glad? If you let yourself be that glad and that forgiving, God will bless you. He will cause the joy of the Holy Spirit to move inside you and get rid of that thing that has been hurting for so long — that ugly little lump of unforgiveness that has spread like cancer to rob you of joy and of health.

God knows us so well, for He made us. He knows even a little unforgiveness, nurtured in our hearts, will greatly harm us physically, emotionally, and spiritually. When we suffer like that, He lays it on the line for us: "Your pain is caused by your unforgiveness. If you don't forgive, then I cannot forgive you. But if you forgive others, I will forgive you, heal you, and set you completely free!"

## 4. How To Raise The Dead

An amazing example of praise at work is when Jesus raised Lazarus from the dead. Jesus was told that Lazarus was ill, but didn't go to him right away. He waited till Lazarus was dead, then told the disciples, ". . . Let's go to Judea." (John 11:7) The disciples didn't want to go. The people in Judea had tried to kill Jesus the last time they were there. Why should they risk their lives going to a funeral!

Jesus then said something that must have sounded strange to the disciples. "Lazarus is dead. And for your sake, I am glad I wasn't there, for this will give you another opportunity to believe in me . . ." (John 11:14,15). Jesus was glad Lazarus was dead. Everybody else considered it a tragedy, but Jesus had another perspective on things and was glad.

When they arrived in Bethany where Lazarus lived, the family, friends, and many prominent Jewish leaders had gathered to mourn the dead. There was wailing and weeping and not much praise and thanksgiving. When they saw Jesus, some got angry and said, ". . . this fellow healed a blind man — why couldn't he keep Lazarus from dying? . . ." (John 11:37)

Jesus was disappointed at their reaction and said, "Where is he buried?" They showed him, and he said, "Roll the stone away!"

Up to that point you or I could probably have done what Jesus did. We could have gone to the funeral, consoled the family, and if we believed what the Bible says, "All things work together for good to them that love God," we might have tried to tell the family it had all happened for the best. But in all likelihood, that is as far as you or I would go, even if we were challenged by the family of the dead; "You say you're a Christian and your God can do anything — how about asking Him to do something now!"

What did Jesus do? Did He ask God for help? Did He plead, "Father, will you hear me, please, because I've got a big problem here and I need help"?

No, He just stood there and said, "Father, I thank You that You've heard me, and that You always hear me." Jesus didn't ask God to do something. He thanked Him that it was already done. He was saying, "Thank you that the problem isn't a problem any more."

There was quite a crowd around the grave, mourning and crying. The disciples were looking over their shoulders, worrying about getting caught and killed. Jesus was the only one there without a problem. He didn't have anything to ask God. He only said, "Thank You, Father, that You always hear me." And then He looked straight at the grave and commanded, "Lazarus, come forth!"

Why can't you and I do the same? Didn't Jesus tell His disciples later, "In solemn truth I tell you, anyone believing in me shall do the same miracles I have done, and even greater ones, because I am going to be with the Father. You can ask Him for *anything,* using my name, and I will do it, for this will bring praise to the Father because of what I, the Son, will do for you. (John 14:12,13)

That is one of the verses in the Bible that often makes us a little uncomfortable. I haven't raised anybody from the dead yet, and you probably haven't either. We can't even handle some of the minor problems that confront us. But Jesus said we could — and He demonstrated how. He simply said, "Father, I thank You that You heard me."

That convinces me that praise and thanksgiving are meant to be the ultimate expression of my confidence and faith in God — that somewhere along the road of learning to thank God for everything, more of His power will be real in our lives. I know the secret is not in the words Jesus said. I could stand before an open coffin and say, "Father, I thank You that You heard me," over and over again, trying a different tone of voice each time. But that wouldn't make the corpse get up. It wasn't how He said it; it was something in the heart of Jesus that flowed directly to the heart of God. If that something could flow through our hearts, the love of God would be released into our lives and the circumstances around us as surely as sunshine flows through an open window to fill a room with warmth and light.

How do we learn to praise God the way Jesus did? I am sure there are different ways to begin, but you've got to start some place, and I started by thanking God for little things, like an old car that wouldn't run. At first if may seem a little silly, but the Bible says that we should be "Giving thanks always for all things . . ." (Eph. 5:20 KJV) That includes old cars, burnt toast, broken tools — everything.

In the beginning I didn't even mean it half the time, but giving thanks was an act of outward obedience to something God wanted me to do. That was the first step for me, and it took quite a long while before I saw many results. The change was gradual. Slowly I began to mean it more when I said, "Thank You"; slowly I began to notice that I was actually happy about some things that always made me upset or unhappy before. Also, I was becoming more convinced that God *was* in charge of everything that happened to me, and it was not so difficult to believe that He brought these circumstances into my life to show me that He loved me.

As I began to share with people and thank God for them in their difficult circumstances, the evidence continued to pile up; praise, as an expression of faith, brought more remarkable results than pleading with God. I found that praise was not just

something I should be doing sometimes. The Bible tells us over
and over that praise is the true expression of worship and love
for God.

But before I understood that much I had to face some
problems. At times praising God got me absolutely nowhere.
Things looked darker than before I began. Depression settled
over me. My words of praise — when I was able to say them —
were empty and without meaning.

What was wrong? I tried new ways of praising. I used my
will to stick with it, even when I wanted to give up. Still there
was no breakthrough. So I finally thanked God for my lack of
joy and lack of faith and asked Him to show me what was
wrong. He showed me that I had reached a point where no
amount of will power, no repeating words of praise, would
bring me any closer to a solution. The problem was not what I
was saying or doing, or even how I was saying or doing it. I was
the problem.

When Jesus said the simple words, "Thank You, Father, for
hearing me," the power of God was instantly released through
Him, because *there was nothing between Jesus and God.*
Nothing in the heart of Jesus blocked His relationship with the
Father. They were one. We know that Jesus prayed for all who
would believe in Him, "I have given them the glory You gave
me — the glorious unity of being one, as we are — I in them
and You in me, all being perfected into one — so that the world
will know You sent me and will understand that You love them
as much as You love me." (John 17:22,23)

Praising God as an act of outward obedience is a good thing,
but it is only a beginning. Sooner or later we come to the point
where our praise seems to break down. That usually means
something more is required of us.

The price is high — and the paying often painful; we must
give up that one thing in our heart that blocks our relationship
with God. Although the reward is oneness with Jesus Christ,
we human beings always resist letting go.

A Jewish ruler asked Jesus what he had to do to be sure of eternal life. "I have kept all the commandments since I was quite young," he said.

But Jesus told him ". . . 'There is still one thing you have missed. Sell everything you possess and give the money away to the poor, and you will have riches in Heaven. Then come and follow me.' But when the man heard this, he was greatly distressed, for he was very rich.

And when Jesus saw how his face fell, he remarked, 'How difficult it is for those who have great possessions to enter the kingdom of God.' " (Luke 18:18,22-24, Phillips)

The problem was not the riches the man owned, but his love for them. Jesus knew what was in the man's heart and put his finger on the one thing that blocked his relationship with God. Anything we will not give up for Jesus is clearly something we consider more important than our relationship with Him. It is a good test-question to ask ourselves, "Is there anything or anyone in my life I won't give up for God or for which I won't thank Him? Is there anyone or anything I won't forgive?" If the answer is yes, that something or someone stands between us and God.

Once a lady told me about her many problems. They included money, health, and family. "I want to turn the whole mess over to God — I have even tried thanking Him for it, but things just get worse. Tell me what I must do to break out of this deadlock."

"Is there anything you know God wants you to do that you *don't* want to do?" I asked.

She blushed and said, "Only one thing I can't forgive — I can't even talk about it."

"That is the one thing God wants you to do before anything else can happen."

She was crying, but her face was set. "Then I'll have to go on suffering — I just can't forgive."

Most of us do a pretty good job of hiding the real issues or denying them. Jeremiah knew something about human nature when he wrote, "The heart is the most deceitful thing there is, and desperately wicked. No one can really know how bad it is! Only the Lord knows! He searches all hearts and examines deepest motives. . ." (Jer. 17:9,10)

David was honest enough to say, "Search me, O God, and know my heart; test my thoughts. Point out anything You find in me that makes You sad, and lead me along the path of everlasting life." (Ps. 139:23,24)

If you pray like that, God will answer. He will remind you of what you are trying to hide. Often His clues are found in the painful circumstances under which we feel so burdened. We can thank Him for them because they aren't meant to punish us, but to bring us closer to Him.

When we know the truth, we must do something about it. "If I regard iniquity in my heart, the Lord will not hear me," (Ps. 66:18 KJV) David said. Anything we hold back from God is sin. As long as we cling to it, He can't hear us. The only remedy for sin is God's forgiveness, and that brings us back to the original basis for our relationship with our Creator; we confess our wrong and surrender it to Him, and He forgives.

As long as I live I will have to depend on His forgiveness. I am more aware of it today than ever before, and I hope I will become even more dependent on it in the future. Are you afraid or ashamed to ask His forgiveness over and over again? Do you think you are playing games with God and that He will get angry or tired of forgiving you? That is not humility. It is your pride that won't let you see how much you depend on God's forgiveness.

One day I stood by the ocean with the waves lapping at my feet. A little boy ran down to the water and filled his play bucket to the brim. Then he ran up on the shore to pour the water into a hole he had dug in the sand. Back and forth he ran, and I suddenly realized that God's forgiveness is as vast as the ocean. We can dip our little buckets again and again, and immediately the water rushes in to replace the little bit we dipped out. No matter how much we take from the ocean, it will be just as full as when we started. And no matter how many bucketfuls we pour into our little hole in the sand, the water will disappear and we will soon need another bucketful.

God's Father heart rejoices when His children come to receive His forgiveness. He does not give it grudgingly and say, "There you are back again. When will you ever learn!" No, each time He sees us come, He says, "I'm so glad you're back, my child. I forgive you and love you."

Our trips back to God, who forgives and forgets, are the lifeline of our fellowship with Him. Each time we honestly admit our wrong and surrender it to Him, Christ is given more control over that area of our lives. The change taking place in us may be gradual or instant, but we can be sure it is happening.

We cannot change ourselves; that is why Paul tells the Ephesians, ". . . be filled instead with the Holy Spirit. . ." (Eph. 5:18) Because ". . . when the Holy Spirit controls our lives, He will produce this kind of fruit in us: love, joy, peace, patience, kindness, goodness, faithfulness, gentleness and self-control . . ." (Gal. 5:22,23) Those are qualities we cannot produce in ourselves.

What does it mean to be filled with the Holy Spirit? It may be easier to understand if we think of it as a process instead of as an instant happening. When Paul said, "*Be* filled . . . ." he used a form of the word that does not exist in English. In the Greek it means something like, "be being filled continually." It is a continuous present tense action word you would use to describe a hose filled with running water. The hose is filled only as long as the water keeps running through it. If the tap is turned off, or something plugs the hose, it is no longer being filled. It is either empty or holding stagnant water.

You and I are like that hose, and we are commanded to be being continually filled with the Holy Spirit, who does not stand still, but is flowing through us. Turning the tap is our continuous attitude of surrender to Christ. Anything that stands between Him and us plugs up the hose. Now do you see how important it is to keep the channel of communication open between God and us? And now do you understand how dependent we are on His continuous forgiveness?

I know that I am not the same person today that I was five years ago, and my relationship with God is not the same as it was then. I hope I have grown and matured some, and that I have surrendered new areas of my life to God so that He has been able to be filling me more with His Holy Spirit. He can only fill me as I am willing to be emptied, and as I am willing to stretch and grow in new areas.

So you and I are like flexible, expandable water hoses, meant to hold more of the Holy Spirit as our relationship with God deepens and grows. A water hose can get clogged up, and so can we. You may be being filled with the Holy Spirit and then you lose your temper, or God shows you something you need to give up, but you refuse. At that point, are you being filled and flowing with the Holy Spirit? Or is the hose plugged?

Some folks talk about a person as "spirit-filled" in reference to a particular experience of surrender to the Holy Spirit. From that point on, they expect the "spirit-filled" person to be nearly perfect. Nothing could be further from the truth. One who has been open to be filled with the Holy Spirit and then plugged up can be more difficult to live with and harder to understand than anyone else. When we have tasted of a close relationship with God and then back away, it is only natural that we become irritable and unhappy. The Holy Spirit brings peace within, and when that peace is gone, we can react very unfavorably to everything and everyone around us.

If we use the term, "I am now being filled with the Holy Spirit," instead of saying, "I am Spirit-filled," we are more accurately describing the way the Holy Spirit works. Paul was carefully directed by the Holy Spirit Himself to use the continuous present tense form of the verb in the Greek. It impressed the early Christians with their need to be continually filled. It isn't a one-time experience, but an on-going process depending on the state of our relationship to God. Are we continuously willing to confess our failings and ask His forgiveness? As we do, we are being emptied of our hang-ups and increasingly filled with Him.

Jesus was continually being filled with the Holy Spirit. He and the Father and the Holy Spirit were one. The picture He used of our relationship with Him was vivid. "Yes, I am the Vine; you are the branches . . . " (John 15:5) Branches cannot grow and produce anything when they are cut off from the vine. They need that life-giving sap flowing through them at all times. It is a picture of complete dependency. The sap, the lifeline, is the Holy Spirit. The more we surrender our lives and ourselves to Him, the more we experience the oneness we are meant to have with Jesus Christ.

True praise springs from a oneness with Christ and acts as a filter turning everything in our lives into joy and thanksgiving. Can you imagine having a praise-filter in your heart? You no longer see pain or problems or tragedy; only wonderful opportunities for God to demonstrate His glory.

Jesus was like that. Not only His tongue, but every fiber of His being was flowing with praise, so He could say at the funeral in Bethany, ". . . I am glad I wasn't there, for this will give you another opportunity to believe in me. . ."

Does part of your life seem dead and buried? Ruined and wasted? Maybe it's your marriage, your business, or your talents. "No use trying to resurrect that," you say. "It's gone forever." You are wrong!

Stop wailing and weeping. Instead say, "I'm *glad* it happened. It's for God's glory!" It is time for resurrection — "Come out, Lazarus!"

## 5. Give Up Your Shackles

A group of practical jokers made a gift for a friend; a heavy iron chain, with a fifty-pound iron ball fastened to one end. They locked the other end around the foot of their buddy, and threw the key away. "Now see how fast you can run," they teased him. Without hesitation the shackled fellow picked up the fifty-pound ball, cradled it in his armpit, and began walking without too much difficulty. "Thanks a lot, fellows," he grinned. "Just what I've always wanted — my very own ball and chain!"

Have you ever met anyone who enjoyed being shackled? Or I'd better ask, do *you* enjoy being shackled? Do you have your very own ball and chain you carry around? In the letter to the Hebrews the writer says, ". . .Let us strip off anything that slows us down or holds us back, and especially those sins that wrap themselves so tightly around our feet and trip us up; . . ." (Hebrews 12:1)

Most of us Christians have put away those obvious, outward sins that are easily seen: theft, murder, adultery. What we haven't given up is usually hidden in our minds and hearts. It might be our attitude toward those who steal, kill, or commit adultery.

Jesus wants to show us that the root of our problem is in the invisible, hidden thoughts of our hearts. He says, "For from the

heart come evil thoughts, murder, adultery, fornication, theft,
lying and slander."(Matt. 15:19)

Like the fellow with the ball and chain, we tell ourselves we
can get along pretty well carrying our extra burden. We say,
"I'm only human and I have my weaknesses, but at least I'm
not as bad as that fellow over there . . . ." We can do that for
awhile, but there comes a day when God will bring our hidden
weakness to our attention in a way we can't ignore.

For years I struggled with immoral thoughts and lustful
dreams. They always made me feel guilty, and I asked God to
forgive me and deliver me from the temptation, but soon I was
right back to where I started. It was a vicious circle, and I
thought I would have to live with it for the rest of my life.

Then one day it came to me that what is most difficult for us
humans is precisely what God wants to do for us. If I really
*wanted* to give up my immoral thoughts, God would take them
and give me Christ's thoughts on the matter instead. "Let this
mind be in you, which was also in Christ Jesus" Paul told the
Phillipians. (Phil. 2:5 KJV)

Of course I said immediately, "You know, God, I *want* to
think only pure thoughts." But then a new idea presented
itself: "Would you be willing to have all your thoughts projected on a screen over your head for everyone to see?"

I felt myself get hot under the collar. What if I wanted to
keep a wrong thought for just a tiny little while before giving it
up? I was suddenly not so sure I was ready to give my thoughts
to God after all.

My problem was no longer a sin I could not stop, but a sin I
was not sure I *wanted* to stop. Before, I had been able to
consider myself a hapless victim of the tempter's snare, and
had pleaded with God to deliver me. Now He was showing me
that I could be delivered in an instant if I wanted. The truth of
James's words burned in my mind: "Temptation is the pull of
man's own evil thoughts and wishes." (James 1:14)

Shamefacedly I had to admit that I actually enjoyed my
hidden thoughts. Surrendering them was not easy. Satan was

busy whispering in my ear that from now on my life would be pretty dull. Finally I was able to say, "Lord, I thank You for all these thoughts that have taught me the truth about myself. Forgive me, Lord. Now take my mind; I surrender it to you, and if you want to project my thoughts on a screen that's all right with me. Only let me have the mind of Christ."

Satan's whispers had been unfounded. They always are. Instead of boredom, I experienced glorious relief, and whenever I saw a pretty girl I was only filled with joy and gratitude. Often tears flowed as I realized the clean, new pleasure God had given me. Now I could appreciate the beauty of God's creation that before had been marred by my own ugly thoughts.

I wanted to share my new freedom with the men in my church and was in my study preparing for the meeting, when suddenly a heavy gloom filled the room. It was as if the devil himself had entered and seemed to say, "Don't you dare talk about that! It's my territory. Keep out!"

When I stood before the men to speak, my throat constricted and the words came with difficulty. But I was able to give the same challenge to them that I had received myself. Many men joined me in surrendering our thoughts to God.

The next day Mary and I flew to Indiana on a speaking tour. There we met our good friends, Gene and Vivian Leak. Gene took me to his farm to see a new piece of equipment: a huge fan used to dry the grain. I leaned down for a closer look. Just then Gene turned on the fan, and a rat that had been hiding inside was shredded into a thousand pieces. The mess spewed over me. As the filth of blood and intestines filled my eyes and nostrils and mouth, and ran down the front of my clean shirt, it seemed I could hear the devil leer in my ear, "That's what you get for intruding on my territory, trying to clean up men's hearts!"

I realized with a burst of joy: Satan can make me filthy on the outside — but Christ has made the inside clean!

Is there something you have tried to give up — but can't? It may be something visible, like alcohol, tobacco, drugs — or less obvious, like too much television watching, reading the wrong literature, or listening to the wrong music. Whatever it is, the problem always originates in your thoughts. Even medical authorities have come to agree with Jesus on that point. They can forcibly remove alcohol, tobacco, drugs, or extra calories from a person, but as long as the "psychological addiction" remains, the person will return to his or her old habits at the first opportunity. "Psychological addiction" is just another term for something which our minds and hearts won't let go.

Be honest with yourself and with God. Do you secretly *enjoy* your weakness? Are you trying to give it up, but at the same time allowing yourself to think or daydream about it? Do you imagine the taste of that banana split or the calming effect of the cigarette?

Do you really want to give it up? Test your sincerity. Can you say to God, "Put my thoughts on a screen if you like, so that my wife and children, my neighbors and friends, can know what I think." When a wrong thought presents itself — and it will just to test you — imagine it projected on that screen. Confess it to God and say, "I've surrendered that thought. I won't think it. Absolutely not!"

Deliberately put your thoughts on something else. As Paul advises, ". . . Fix your thoughts on what is true and good and right. Think about things that are pure and lovely, and dwell on the fine, good things in others. Think about all you can praise God for and be glad about." (Phil. 4:8)

When God sees your wholehearted willingness to let go of the thing that shackles you, He will strengthen your faith to carry it through. A man in our church struggled to give up his cigarette habit. One day he realized that God was telling him, "No more delay. I have been patient for a long time, but today is the day I want you to quit." The man was in his car on the way to church, but pulled over and stopped alongside the road. He bowed his head and prayed, "Lord, I want to know if it is really you telling me, because if it is, I know you can heal me of my habit when I surrender it to you." He sat quietly with his head bowed, thinking, "Lord, I sure would like a sign if it is You talking."

Just then a highway patrol car pulled up, and the officer came over to the man's car. There was nothing unusual in that, but the officer asked, "Are you praying, sir?" When the man nodded, the highway patrol man said quietly, "Would you mind if I got in your car and prayed with you?" Was that a coincidence?

God does not give signs to everybody, but He often does when our faith is weak but our heart is willing. Signs are not given to convince us of God's power, but they may be given to encourage us when we have already decided to believe.

If we give ourselves the 'screen test' and decide we don't want to give up our secret thoughts, we can no longer make-believe that our problem is a sin that won't let us go — we know we are the ones who won't let go of the sin. With the truth unmasked, our refusal to surrender becomes a more serious thing. ". . . you are saving up terrible punishment for yourselves because of your stubbornness in refusing to turn from your sin; . . ." (Rom. 2:5)

It was the British author, C.S. Lewis, who said, "God whispers to us in our pleasures, speaks in our conscience, but shouts in our pain; it is His megaphone to rouse a deaf world." If God can't get our attention any other way, He resorts to harder measures than just speaking softly.

Is the Almighty troubling you? Shouting to you through pain? Are you grateful for it? David was. "It is good for me that I have been afflicted; that I might learn thy statutes." (Ps. 119:71 KJV) Is it difficult to understand that God afflicts us because He loves us? The writer to the Hebrews says, ". . . And have you quite forgotten the encouraging words God spoke to you, His child? He said, 'My son, don't be angry when the Lord punishes you. Don't be discouraged when he has to show you where you are wrong. For when He punishes you, it proves that

He loves you. When He whips you it proves you are really His child.' " (Heb. 12:5,6)

I used to think those were hard, unreasonable words. But I have experienced some of God's 'chastenings' in my own life, and have come to realize that God troubles me because He loves me too much to let me continue in my rebellion apart from Him. My heart's desire is to experience a oneness with Jesus Christ. If God has to put me in pain or difficult circumstances to bring me closer, I can only praise and thank Him for the things that hurt enough to get and keep my attention.

Not long ago I received a letter from a couple who had asked us to pray for their son who was awaiting trial for robbery. The boy had left home when he was eighteen because he did not agree with his parents' rules. At first they had grieved and worried, but someone gave them *Prison to Praise,* and they decided to surrender their worries and their son to God, and thank Him for every circumstance He brought into their son's life.

Not long after that, their son came on the scene of a robbery, and was shot and arrested for the crime. He lost an eye in the shooting, but he maintained his innocence and demanded a jury trial. It was while waiting for the trial that he surrendered his life to God.

In the letter his parents told how he had been found innocent and was now home with them, rejoicing that God had spared his life for a special reason. "He is forever saying, 'Thank God I lost the eye' — 'It is better to lose one eye than that my whole body should be lost in hell!' " (See Matt. 5:29)

God does not often resort to such means to get our attention. But if He must in order to save us from total destruction, we have reason to rejoice. Our pain or trial is a demonstration of God's love for us. He wants us to be set free from every little sin that wraps itself around our feet, threatening to trip us up and keep us from oneness with our heavenly Father.

One of the most subtle sins that entangles us is an attitude of criticism. I believe it causes more unhappiness than all the physical diseases put together. It breaks up marriages, chases children away from home, and splits groups. People become physically ill because they have been so wounded in their souls by constant fault-finding. Some withdraw into mental illness; others commit crimes or turn to alcohol, drugs, or overeating, or become social misfits or chronic failures because they have been told over and over again that everything they do is wrong.

Our entire society is marred by the deadly poison of criticism. It permeates homes, classrooms, churches, mass-media, politics, and international affairs.

We all know how a critical remark can spoil our entire day, yet those who make the criticisms usually feel they are right to do it. We criticize, we tell ourselves, only because we want to tell the truth and be helpful!

I have received thousands of letters that illustrate the point. Here is one:

Dear Rev. Carothers:

My husband only came to church when I begged him, and one day I discovered that he was smoking in secret. I told him over and over how wrong it was to smoke, but he wouldn't listen. Then my mother gave me *Prison to Praise*. I decided to try thanking God for my husband's habit instead of complaining about it. That is when I discovered I had a habit of my own. Every day I watched television soap operas for an hour. I wouldn't let anything keep me from seeing 'my' programs! What right did I have to criticize my husband when I was just as 'hooked' myself? I surrendered my habit to God and started spending that hour every day in prayer and thanksgiving for my husband. Within a week he came home to say he had given up smoking and turned himself over to God!"

Most of the letters I get have a happy ending, but I have in my files others that tell of futile attempts to pray and praise — where in the end a husband or a wife or a child left home or remained in the clutches of alcohol or drugs. Often a bitter, critical, or mournful attitude in the letter made it easy to understand why.

Jesus called criticism murder. He also said, ". . . Let the one among you who has never sinned throw the first stone. . . ." (John 8:7 Phillips) Negative, critical, fault-finding words can destroy someone as effectively as throwing stones.

Criticism is dangerous to those who practice it. Jesus said, "Don't criticize people, and you will not be criticized. For you will be judged by the way you criticize others, and the measure you give will be the measure you receive." (Matt. 7:1-2 Phillips)

Other people's sin is likened to a speck of sawdust, and our critical attitude is the plank. The more we talk or think about other people's faults or failures and try to set them straight, the more we become guilty ourselves.

Only by allowing God to remove our plank, do we become fit to help our brother with his little speck. The goal is to get rid of both the plank and the speck — but in that order.

Admitting our critical attitude is the first step, but that isn't easy. Fault-finding is an ingrained habit with most of us. When we look at others, the first thought that pops into our head is usually negative. We tend to think of others as needing God's forgiveness more than we do — a sure sign that a plank of criticism protrudes from our eye. Beyond the circle of our family and closest associates we often hide our critical thoughts behind flattering words to those we don't like. "They speak vanity, every one with his neighbor: with flattering lips and a double heart do they speak." (Ps 12:2, KJV) Try to imagine that everyone you speak to can see what you think about them projected on a screen over your head. That would quickly unmask our critical attitude, wouldn't it!

Nowhere is the damage of criticism as obvious as in millions of homes that have been turned into disaster areas by ugly words and attitudes. We seem to hurt most the ones we claim to love. Every day I hear from people who want to tell me what is wrong with the other members of their family. My answer is, "God wants to heal your family, and He can start with you if you are willing to stop criticizing and start being thankful for your family the way it is."

Our critical attitude must be seen as the horrible sin it really is. We must ask God to forgive us and surrender our thoughts to Him. He can fill us with love for those of whom we have been critical. Then when a fault-finding thought comes into our head we must refuse to hang onto it, and instead, follow Paul's advice, ". . . Dwell on the fine, good things in others." (Phil. 4:8)

Once we start thinking about the good points in others, it is surprising how soon we begin to admire them and appreciate them and thank God for them exactly as they are. Soon their faults won't look half so bad as they once seemed. With our attitude changed, God can reach down and remove any little speck that may still remain in our brother's eye as well.

With our critical thoughts surrendered to God, we must give Him our tongue as well and ask Him to control it. How many times have you said things you wish you hadn't? The tongue has put people in trouble since the beginning of time. ". . . The tongue is a small thing, but what enormous damage it can do. . . . And the tongue is set on fire by hell itself, and can turn our whole lives into a blazing flame of destruction and disaster . . . but no human being can tame the tongue. It is always ready to pour out its deadly poison." (James 3:5,6,8)

Well-meaning parents feel compelled to give their teenage children the same good advice over and over again, even if they know it does no good. Do they also know that in ninety-nine percent of the cases their talking only makes Johnny worse? The disastrous effect of too many words — however well meant — is most apparent in family relationships, but we do the same

thing with our friends, on the job, on the telephone, and in the
pulpit. Christians who over-talk have turned many people
from God.

It is possible to say good and true things and still be wrong
in saying them. "Speak not in the ears of a fool: for he will
despise the wisdom of thy words." (Prov. 23:9 KJV) Perhaps a
fool needs to be told a thing or two, but as long as he won't
listen, you are wrong in telling him.

The compulsion to tell others what we think they ought to
know does not come from God, but from our attitude of
self-righteous criticism, and every word we speak to "set them
straight" sows resentment, hurt and discord. Jesus never
over-talked. He knew when to speak and when to demonstrate
His love in other ways. He told His followers, "I tell you that
men will have to answer at the day of judgment for every
careless word they utter — for it is your words that will acquit
you, and your words that will condemn you!" (Matt. 12:36,37
Phillips) Can you imagine standing face-to-face with God and
have an instant replay of every careless and idle word you've
ever spoken? It is a sobering thought.

"If anyone can control his tongue, it proves he has perfect
control over himself in every other way." (James 3:2) If we let
our mouths run off with anything that comes into our heads,
our actions are probably just as undisciplined.

Are you a person of few words? If you don't know, maybe
you should ask an honest friend. Most of us are unaware that
we let our mouths run. But others notice — our talkativeness
may hurt them or bore them, and our flood of words may
obscure what we really want to say. God gave us the ability to
think and speak in the first place so that we could communi-
cate with Him and with others, but most of us have misused
this wonderful privilege.

Whether you are a person of few or many words, if you have
misused them, God forgives you. He can change our critical or
depressing words into loving, encouraging words. Our rambling
chatter or helpless stutterings can become meaningful, clear

expressions. Let David's prayer become yours: "Let the words of my mouth, and the meditation of my heart, be acceptable in thy sight, O Lord, my strength, and my redeemer." (Ps. 19:14 KJV)

Surrender your tongue to God — ask Him to tame and use it. When the urge to speak comes over you, ask, "God, is what I want to say really necessary?" If we quietly wait on God, He will give us the right words to say — kind, encouraging, uplifting words, speaking directly to people's needs in a way we could never do with our normal intelligence.

Once a lady wrote me an angry letter saying that I should not waste my time writing stupid books. She said she had been foolish enough to try praising God, but it didn't work. Her child had been born mentally retarded, and all the prayers and praising did nothing to change her condition. "So why do you waste your time telling these ridiculous stories?" she wrote.

I could have written back thousands of words trying to explain how she had misunderstood my books. Instead, I asked God if there was something I could say that would help her. In my mind's eye I "saw" a picture of a pregnant woman going shopping, falling down, and hurting herself. I saw her husband angry because she had gone out alone. When the baby was born mentally retarded, the husband placed all the blame on his wife.

The picture was so vivid that I described it in my letter to the lady. She replied immediately. I had told her exactly what had happened, and it convinced her that God really cared and knew all about her situation. It wasn't my intelligence or superior way with words that impressed her, but something God showed me, and I passed it on to her.

Think of what it can do if we let God control our tongues. Then the people we speak to will pick up their ears instead of turning us off. God will be speaking through us, and they will hear Him.

From now on you can be someone who always lifts up people by the way you speak. When they see you coming they will be glad, because they know you always have a kind and loving word. Your husband hurries home, your wife can't wait to see you, your children bring their friends home after school — because your home is a warm and loving place, and you always speak good things about others. Your fellow workers, your friends, or your customers seek you out, because your words brighten their day instead of depressing them.

The oneness Christ promised becomes more and more real as we surrender our hidden sins, our thoughts and our words to Him. The Holy Spirit can continuously be filling these new areas of our lives. With cleansed heart and yielded tongue, praise takes on a richer, deeper meaning. Now we can join David in saying, "I will praise thee with uprightness of heart, when I shall have learned thy righteous judgments." (Ps. 119:7) "Be glad in the Lord, and rejoice, ye righteous: and shout for joy, all ye that are upright in heart." (Ps. 32:11 KJV)

Righteousness and uprightness are conditions for true praise, but we can never achieve them on our own. They are God's generous gift to a repentant heart.

## 6. *What Is Your Strength?*

Good things can come between us and God, making true praise impossible. They may not be the same things in my life as in yours, but they can be identified by asking a few questions:

What do you think you *have* to have in order to be happy and live successfully? Most Christians will answer quickly, "Jesus Christ, of course." But is Jesus *all* you need? You may say "Yes," but are you acting as if deep down you believe you need Jesus *plus* something? What about the people you love? Do you ever worry about losing them? What about your job? Are you concerned about having enough money to pay the bills? What about your health, your strength or your talents? Would losing them upset you?

We often are not aware that we rely on something other than God until that something is taken from us. One of the most joyful Christians I ever met is Miriam Peterson. She grew up as an only child, adored by her parents, and married a man who loved her with deep devotion. They had three bright and beautiful children, enjoyed financial security, and a large circle of friends. Neither Miriam nor her husband thought about God. Religion was unimportant until Steve, their teenage son, who had been the apple of his father's eye, suddenly became rebellious. Miriam could not understand what had gone wrong and thought perhaps she had failed as a mother.

For the first time in her life she prayed that God, if He was real, would in some way reveal Himself to her.

Surprisingly, Miriam's husband made the suggestion that they should start attending church. She began to read the Bible and took her first step in faith towards Jesus Christ. Shortly after that, it seemed as if the very fabric of their well-ordered life came apart. Their oldest son, John, started using drugs, and while he was high, beat his girl friend's baby, so that the child later died. John was arrested. Steve was also taking drugs and drifted from one eastern cult to another. Miriam was horrified, and the thought hounded her, "I did not teach my children to love Christ." Driven by guilt, she sought God's forgiveness, and studied her Bible diligently for a better understanding of His Word.

While John was in prison, Miriam's husband died. Steve, who had been arrested for drugs, jumped bail and fled to Europe. Miriam's former friends, shocked that such tragedies could happen to a "good family," rallied around her, but she felt as if she could not endure a moment longer of the nightmare her life had become. Her heart cried out, "Why, God, why?"

Someone gave her *Prison to Praise* and, nearly numbed by fear and anguish, she thought, "What can I lose?" At the end of her rope, she began to thank God for everything that had happened. John had been released from prison, but suffered violent temper tantrums. Psychiatric treatment did not help. One morning he woke his mother to tell her he intended to murder his girl friend and then commit suicide. To demonstrate how strongly he felt, he went through the house knocking over lamps and furniture. Miriam handed him the book *Prison to Praise* and said, "There might be something here that can save both of us."

She came home from work to find John a changed person. He had surrendered himself to God and found forgiveness and peace. Before long, Steve called from Switzerland and told a remarkable story. He had been penniless on a snowy, cold night, when the cook at an inn gave him some food and a place to sleep. Late that night the innkeeper discovered his presence and threw him out in below freezing weather. Steve had few clothes and nowhere to go. Thinking he would be dead before morning, he saw that his entire life had come to nothing. He threw himself down in the snow, and for the first time in his life prayed, "God, if you are real, please help me."

In that moment Steve suddenly knew that Christ was real, and that He had come to save him. With tears of repentance and joy, he asked Jesus to take over his life. Then he got up and started to walk through the snow. Soon he found an abandoned automobile. He climbed inside and spent the night thanking God for saving his life. After calling his mother, he started on his way back to Paris. Working at odd jobs, he saved enough money for the trip home. There he faced up to the charges still pending against him, and was soon completely free.

Miriam is radiant when she tells what God is doing in the lives of her sons, who are both working with young people in our church. But her joy is no less apparent as she recounts the tragic moments God put her through. David wrote, "Make us glad according to the days wherein thou hast afflicted us, and the years wherein we have seen evil." (Ps. 90:15 KJV)

Through those days of pain Miriam discovered the joy and gladness of depending only on God. "I used to depend on my family, and on the friends who surrounded me constantly," she says. "When God removed them all, I learned that I needed only Him to be happy."

Before the trials piled into her life, she thought of herself as a happy, fun-loving person. "But it was only surface deep," she told me. "If anything went wrong, my day was ruined, and I plunged into depression and worry."

With a happy smile, she continued, "My duty is not to worry, but to praise God in everything!"

One day recently she dropped twenty pounds of dogfood on a brand-new shag rug. "I wasn't upset at all," she laughed. "All I

could think to say was, 'Praise the Lord!' — the old me would
have gone into hysterics."

Miriam still has problems with her third child, and once,
during a particular crisis, she worried about it for nearly a
whole day. "But I knew every minute that my worry only
saddened God, who was in charge."

Today Miriam is surrounded by a loving family and friends.
But she is not dependent on them any longer. Jesus Christ is
*all* she needs. Once we know that — all else can be ours in the
measure God knows we should have it to be truly happy in
Him.

Right now our country and the entire world are going
through perilous economic times. Even the most experienced
observers dare not speak with certainty about what lies ahead.
I believe God is bringing this upon us to give us the opportunity to depend on Him for our financial security. How else would
we learn?

Are the times troubling you? Are you concerned about the
value of your property? Your family's future? If you are, it
indicates that you think you need money to be secure more
than you need God.

A man wrote me to say that he had worked very hard all his
life to make ends meet, but somehow his bills always exceeded
his paycheck. Working overtime did no good, and he lived with
a growing fear that one day he would not be able to keep up
with the demands of his creditors.

Someone gave him a book on praise, and it caused him to
see that there was something wrong with the way he was
trying to cope with his situation. He determined to praise God
for every bill, and sat down to write a check for the most urgent
one. "I looked at the little piece of paper in front of me and said,
"Thank you, God, for this bill. Bless the check and people who
receive it." It occured to him that stamps and envelopes had
cost money, too, so he asked God to bless the people from whom
he had bought them. Then he noticed the lamp on his desk and
said, "God bless the people who send me the electric bill." Next

he asked God to bless the people who held the mortgage on his house, and those who had received the money for the desk and chair in which he was sitting.

"Those who collected my taxes needed blessings, too," he wrote. "On and on I went, and I suddenly realized that always before I had cursed these people for taking my money. Now I felt really grateful for that first check ready to go in the mail. Asking God to bless it had lifted my gloom and my worries."

Within a week the man got a letter back from that first creditor, stating that they had made a mistake on their bill. He did not owe them any money, they owed him! In the letter was his own check back and another one made out for the same amount. Nothing like that had ever happened before. He prayed for wisdom to use the money, and realized that the two checks put together would make a nice dent in an old debt. He had received several letters reminding him what he owed, so he knew his money would not be returned this time. Off went his check with another "Bless them, Lord."

By return mail came a letter from the company asking him to come down to their store so that they could give him a special prize, since he had been the first to respond to their recent letter. He had not received any correspondence from them recently, and thought the invitation was a gimmick to get him to buy something more now that he was paying on his old bill.

Then he remembered how he had gotten the money to pay the bill in the first place, and decided to go to the store after all. A polite secretary explained that they had offered special prizes to anyone who paid on an account a year or more overdue. He had been the first, and they asked permission to take his picture and record the ceremony in the local newspaper to encourage others to pay their bills.

What was the prize? The man nearly fell over when they told him, "Ten times the amount you paid on your bills!"

"Now I had twenty times the amount for which I wrote the first check. I took the new check and went home to ask God to bless it. There were several other bills that needed to be paid, and I asked for wisdom to know how to use the money. The answer shook me. I felt God wanted me to give it away! That would not help my situation at all. I was still deep in debt, but no matter how I prayed, all I could think of was, 'Give it away!' "

Finally the man called his pastor and said he had a gift for the church. When he mentioned the amount, the pastor thanked him for responding so quickly to the need.

"What need?"

"The one I announced in church last Sunday for that exact amount."

The man had not been in church that Sunday, and had not heard about the pastor's plea. Now he was convinced that God was in charge of his money. He continued to ask His blessing on every bill and every check he wrote. In the letter to me he enclosed a substantial donation to our prison ministry, and concluded by saying that God prospered him in everything, so that he was now looking for new ways to invest what God is giving him.

Would God do the same for you if you started to praise Him for your bills? It is quite possible, if one important condition is met in your heart. Praising God became a turning point for this man because it was a demonstration of an inward surrender of his finances. The proof was his willingness to follow God's instructions in handling his money.

God may not make you rich — but you never have to worry about money as long as you realize that every penny comes from God and belongs to Him. Use it as He directs, and your needs will always be met, regardless of the state of the world economy. Paul wrote, ". . . I have learned the secret of facing either plenty or poverty. I am ready for anything through the strength of the one who lives within me." (Phil. 4:12,13 Phillips)

Paul's secret was that he had discovered from where his real strength came — not from money or friends or his own efforts, but from Christ. He *is* our strength.

A prisoner wrote me who had struggled to be a Christian for some time. In spite of his efforts, he slipped into what he called, "a horribly backslidden condition." He gave up prayer and Bible study, and was learning about witchcraft. He finally reached a point where he saw his life without meaning. He wrote, "I hated to admit my own inability to help myself, but it was at that point that Jesus came to lift me up to His strength. Pride had kept me from accepting Him before, but when I reached the bottom I had nothing left of which to be proud. I am glad God brought me down so I could see the truth and His wonderful grace."

From my vantage point as a pastor, I hear from people every day who say things like, "I tried all my life to do the right thing, but failed. When I gave up struggling and accepted whatever God wanted to do with me, something glorious happened. I gave up trying in my own strength and experienced God's strength."

Our own strength, no matter how strong we are, is never enough. It will never be right. And when we learn that we can never be right, never be strong enough, no matter how hard we try, we finally understand that we have to depend on Jesus to do it for us. That glorious discovery sets us free at last from our own self-efforts, and we are free to receive all that God wants to give us.

The stronger and more capable we are, the harder it can be to see our need for God. He may have to bring about circumstances in our lives to destroy our illusion of self-sufficiency.

Tom Silsby was a tall and exceptionally good-looking high school student. His unusually broad shoulders and magnificent physique made him the envy of nearly every boy who knew him. He was a star athlete who won every competition he entered. His parents were Christians, but from his sophomore year, Tom slowly drifted away from his own faith. He was convinced he did not need God. His own strength and skill made him both feared and admired by other students. By the time Tom became a senior, he was a heavy week-end drinker and a bully who enjoyed pushing others around. He made his money by fixing up old cars and selling them for a high profit, and his goal in life was to be a big-shot. Already his picture was featured regularly in the sports pages of the newspapers; Tom was a star football player, champion wrestler, and swimmer.

Early one morning he was on his way home after an all-night party. His little VW convertible was going too fast down the freeway, when Tom nodded behind the wheel, and the car spun out of control and went over a 300-foot cliff embankment.

At the hospital the cuts on Tom's face and back were stitched, along with a deep gash in his skull. No bones were broken, but he was in a deep coma, and tests revealed severe brain and brain stem damage. A team of surgeons operated, but held little hope for complete recovery.

In the meantime, Tom's parents and family, their pastors, and Christians in churches near and far joined in committing Tom and his future into God's hands. The parents were firm in their faith that God would heal their son. Tom himself hung between unconsciousness and semi-consciousness for several weeks. When he was awake he recognized his parents, but his memory was gone, and he could only speak a few, halting words. The doctors felt doubtful that he would ever regain the full use of his mind or his left side.

Tom spent five weeks in a rehabilitation ward, learning to sit up by himself, to eat, even to stand for a few minutes, but his mind was that of a small child. Snatches of memory were coming back, but everything he had learned before was gone. Still, the prayers continued. His parents held to their belief that God was healing Tom, and they rejoiced as they brought him home.

Now began a long, persistent struggle for Tom to relearn what he had once known. Encouraged by his parents, he started exercising, weight-lifting, running, and then swimming. At first he stumbled and fell whenever he tried to run, because one leg was weaker than the other. In the swimming pool he first splashed the water with his hands and giggled like a small child. When he tried to swim, he sank to the bottom and his father had to pull him out.

Slowly Tom was regaining some of his physical abilities, but his mind was still operating on the fifth-grade level, and he had poor recall of the past. His parents told him he could make it if he learned to rely on Christ's strength instead of his own. Tom agreed.

Now began a series of humiliating experiences for the former star athlete. Tom was allowed back on the swimming team, but he had to work hard just to complete the race instead of winning it. In wrestling he was thrown to the floor by guys much smaller than himself. He was accepted back on the football team by his old coach and team mates, who admired his persistence, but everything he had once known about football was forgotten. His old, rough friends laughed at his clumsiness. When he was admitted to junior college he was at the very bottom of his class.

But it was through those humiliating experiences that the presence of Jesus became real to Tom. In his own helplessness he discovered that the strength of Jesus was something reliable. "I've learned to put Jesus first," he says. "And I have learned that just as I need a coach and a team to become a good athlete, I also need a pastor and fellowship to grow in Christ. Athletic games have rules, and often the coach has to explain them over and over before I finally can apply the principle to the game. As Christians we have the Big Coach and the Big Rule Book. Some things in there I don't know how to apply to life, but the Big Coach patiently explains it to me, and I know that one day I will understand more of it."

Tom is doing well in school today, and instead of the clumsy searching for words, he expresses himself clearly. He spends much time working with young people in the church, and is much admired and loved for his quiet, kind disposition. He is very different from the rough bully he once was.

"I almost died," he says, "but God gave me real life. Before, I had everything I thought I wanted. I was big and strong and successful. I got everything I reached out for, and I woke up every morning wondering what I could do to make me enjoy that day more.

I was a winner in the eyes of the world, but it was by losing, that I became a real winner. God took away everything to show me that only He can give me what is really important. I have learned that the secret of life is in receiving from God rather than in trying to take what you can get!"

Tom does not find it difficult to agree with David, who wrote, "Make me to hear joy and gladness; that the bones which thou hast broken may rejoice." (Ps. 51:8 KJV)

When God breaks our bones, it is because He wants us to discover the joy and gladness we find when we rely on His strength.

Shifting from our own strength to God's does not come easy to any of us. We may rely on Him in one area, but not in another — or we trust Him more in some things than in others. Turning ourselves over to Him completely is a life-time process. We think we have done it, and up pops that old ego, still trying to run the show our old way.

It is easier to say, "The Lord is my strength," than to live that way. The last few years our church in Escondido and the Foundation of Praise have grown very quickly. With each new book, the pile of letters from readers mount higher, and phone calls, visits, and requests for personal appearances pour into our offices. I believe that everyone who comes asking for help is sent by Him. So when the number of calls and letters grew larger than I could handle, I began to feel guilty because I couldn't help everybody.

For months I struggled with the growing pressure. My guilt grew worse when we got an unlisted phone number at home, but the calls had kept me up all hours of the night. I cried to

God for more strength, but, instead, my exhaustion grew, and my wife and co-workers began to be concerned for my health. I continually thanked God for every call and letter, while I asked Him to forgive me for not being able to answer them all — yet somehow my guilt was never quite relieved. Finally there was nothing left to do but give up trying to handle it all. I said, "Lord, I am so sorry I can't take care of all the people you send me. You'll have to meet their needs some other way . . ."

There was a long silence, then I felt the Lord saying, "I'm glad you finally realize I can get some of these things done without you, Merlin."

"Why, Lord, of course I know you can do things without me . . ."

"Then why do you act as if you are personally responsible for helping those people? Don't you know they need Me more than they need Merlin Carothers?"

My own sin suddenly stared me in the face. For years I had been saying that it was Jesus, not Merlin Carothers, who helped the people to whom 'I' ministered. I had prayed, "Lord, use me to your glory, not my own." Yet somewhere, deep in the hidden recesses of my heart, I had been taking some of that glory. I had been operating in some of my own strength. The problem was pride, and my guilt and exhaustion were dead give-aways.

God may be flashing the same warning signals in your face. If you are doing what you think God wants you to do, yet you feel guilty because you aren't doing enough, and you're tired because the workload is growing; ask yourself, "Could God use someone else in my place and do it just as well?" If that nudges your pride just a bit, and you are not absolutely sure God could operate as well without you — watch out!

Confessing my sin, I could finally say, "You are my strength, Lord. Use me only where You want me — and thank You for all the work You are going to do through others."

The guilt and pressure were gone, and others began to respond to the need. Today we have a 24-hour telephone life line manned by volunteers. Over one hundred and fifty deacons and assistant shepherds and shepherdesses do the work of helping and encouraging our own congregation and the many who come to us for assistance. I have seven assistant pastors and an administrator. There are six full-time secretaries in the office and seven hundred volunteer correspondents who answer letters from prisoners all over the United States and several other countries.

Now that millions have read my books, it often happens that people who are desperate call me to say, "If only you will pray for me, I know God will do something." It is always a little frightening to hear people say things like that, because it means they believe I can do something that only God can do. God does not need Merlin Carothers to spread the word about Praise or to pray for people. If I thought He did, I would be in danger of leading thousands of people to depend on me instead of Jesus.

A certain pastor took over a small struggling church, and the members multiplied several times over in just a few months. The pastor was immensely popular, and the church prospered, but after two years the pastor was called away. As quickly as the congregation had grown, it now dwindled, and the church closed its doors. The explanation given was: "Pastor so-and-so had such a wonderful personality — we couldn't find anyone to take his place."

Who had the largest following in that church? The popular pastor or Jesus? Who do people respond to when you are around — Christ in you — or just plain you?

I still struggle with the problem of how to speak at all the places to which I am asked to speak throughout the United States and the world. My schedule has been too heavy, and God has let my health suffer under it. I am getting the message slowly. Thank God He won't let me get away with operating in my own strength — not even a little bit — because that masks my hidden pride. Crying for more strength won't work, nor will all my maneuvering. Steadfastly He will wait until I am ready to surrender it all and say, "Lord, I give up my own strength. I have *no* strength. You are my strength, and I thank you for all the places you will use other speakers than Merlin Carothers."

It isn't easy to say that, because I enjoy speaking. I love to be a part of God's work. But I know it is *His* work, not mine, and it will go on long after I am gone, just as it began long before I got here.

How do we get to the point where God is all our strength? As long as we use our own strength, God cannot use His through us. Only when we surrender our strength will we discover what David meant when he said, "Blessed is the man whose strength is in Thee . . ." (Ps. 84:5 KJV)

Benjamin Franklin said, "The Lord helps those who help themselves." But nothing could be farther from the truth. The Lord helps those who are helpless. But it isn't enough to be helpless; we have to *give up* trying to help ourselves and surrender to God.

Our own strength is only a false illusion; still we cling to it and hate to give it up. If we want God to be our strength, we must be able to say to Him, "I surrender all my own strength to You. From now on I want You to be my *only* strength."

If you say that and then find yourself getting more and more tired — praise God! He is letting you wear out your own strength, and when it is all gone, you will be where you ought to be — dependent on God for everything. At last you can say with David, "The Lord is my strength and my shield; my heart trusted in Him and I am helped: therefore my heart greatly rejoiceth; and with my song will I praise Him." (Ps. 28:7 KJV)

# 7. Keep Your Eyes Steady!

When your eyes are examined, the doctor holds a card in front of you and says, "Keep your eyes here, but tell me when you see my other hand." Then he brings his hand from behind your head and pretty soon, out of the corner of your eye, you see his hand. You are still looking straight ahead at the card, but you also see that hand.

That is a capacity God has given our physical eyes, and also our spiritual vision. We can be looking at Christ, and at the same time, out of the corner of our eyes, there is something else trying to catch our attention. Now it is up to us. We can focus our full attention on Christ, disregarding the disturbance on the side — or shift our attention over to the other — or do like most of us, hesitate somewhere in between, looking back and forth, and not being able to decide one way or the other.

If you are in the last category, you are what James described: "A double-minded man is unstable in all his ways, let not that man think that he shall receive anything of the Lord." (See James 1:8,7.) No one is more miserable than a double-minded or double-hearted human being. Sometimes you're convinced you believe God, and the next day you don't know for sure.

Jesus said, ". . . When your eye is single, thy whole body also is full of light; but when thine eye is evil, thy body also is full of darkness." (Luke 11:34 KJV) Jesus is saying that to doubt, and to divide our attention between God and something else is evil. Those may seem like hard words, but remember that the first and great commandment Jesus gives us is, "Thou shalt love the Lord thy God with *all* thy heart, and with *all* thy soul, and with *all* thy mind." (Matt. 22:37)

To be double-minded or double-hearted is a miserable condition of uncertainty, and sinful as well. God said of the Israelites, ". . . I was very angry with them, for their hearts were always looking somewhere else instead of up to me . . ." (Heb. 3:10) God had promised the Israelites a beautiful land flowing with milk and honey, if they had only kept looking to Him. But they ruined their chances and lost the Promised Land by looking elsewhere.

What causes double mindedness? What do you see out of the corner of your eye that compels you to look away from Christ? One of the biggest attention getters is our physical body. Since we were born we have responded to what our body tells us about ourselves. We feel hungry, warm, cold, weak, strong, in pain, sleepy, full of lust — and our mind is used to translating these feelings into "facts." We think we are what we feel, and that we must do what our feelings dictate.

When we become Christians, the Holy Spirit enters our body and there is a new voice in our life. The Spirit speaks in our thoughts, usually in direct disagreement with our feelings. Suddenly we have a battle going on inside us.

This is the origin of our double-mindedness. Every born-again Christian starts his new life with a double mind. Our soul is a battleground where Jesus Christ has won the decisive victory, but each of us must "Fight the worthwhile battle of the faith" (I Tim. 6:12 Phillips) till our attention is focused on God with a single mind and a united heart.

Many do not realize their own double-mindedness. They assume that every thought originates in their own head. Once we are alerted to our true condition, we can begin to sort out what we are thinking. We are powerless to stop the thoughts from popping into our heads, but God has given us the power to decide what to do with them once they are there.

". . . We have no particular reason to feel grateful to our sensual nature, or to live life on the level of the instincts. Indeed that way of living leads to certain spiritual death. But if on the other hand, you cut the nerve of your instinctive actions by obeying the Spirit, you are on the way to real living." (Rom. 8:12,13 Phillips)

We cut the nerve of our instinctive action by deciding in favor of God's voice against our feelings and thoughts. We don't have the power to resist the pull of our old instincts, but as we surrender to God and fasten our sight on Christ, His power overcomes our old nature.

In sorting out our thoughts we should recognize that Satan always appeals to our old nature and stirs up our feelings, while the Holy Spirit tells us what God's Word says. We are then faced with the familiar situation from the doctor's office. The Holy Spirit says, "Look this way, here is what God has to say. Keep your eyes focused on Jesus." Now Satan comes up from the rear and whispers, "God doesn't care about your situation. You don't *feel* His presence do you?"

What are you going to do? Will you waver and say, "N-n-no, I don't feel anything. Maybe God left me . . ."? Or will you confess your double-mindedness and decide to believe God's Word no matter what you feel or don't feel?

The Holy Spirit tells us that in Christ we have His perfect peace. (John 14:27) But our circumstances are so miserable that we feel far from peaceful. What can we do about it? Our old nature will blame our circumstances for our lack of peace, but God's Word tells us that if we tell God every detail of our needs in thankful prayer and don't worry, the peace of God that passes human understanding will keep constant guard over our hearts and minds as they rest in Christ Jesus. (Phil. 4:6,7) The promise is that we will have perfect peace as our hearts and minds are focused on Jesus — not on our circumstances.

Isn't it wonderful that we have the freedom in Christ to choose *not* to let the circumstances and our feelings rule our lives? Doesn't that give us reason to shout for joy and praise God?

Whatever your particular weakness, that is where your old feelings will act up, telling you that you are still the same old person. God's Word says that you are a new creature in Christ. (II Cor. 5:17) Who are you going to believe?

Each time we cut the nerve of our instinctive action by obeying the Spirit and surrendering our old feelings to God, our double-mindedness is being replaced with faith. And faith is the quality that enables us to say, "God, I believe You, even if my senses and my feelings tell me the opposite."

The more we waver between two opinions, the less faith we have. We say, "God, if you would just let me *feel* good for a change, or see a miracle with my own eyes, it would be so much easier to believe." We don't have to use faith when we see or feel a miracle. The opportunity to practice faith comes when things go wrong and we feel bad.

The Holy Spirit says, "Always be full of joy in the Lord; . . ." (Phil. 4:4) That sounds impossible, because after all, joy is something we can *feel,* isn't it? But we are commanded to be filled with joy, and God doesn't command something that can't be done. So it must be possible to be joyful always — regardless of circumstances.

We are used to thinking that happy circumstances bring joy, but God wants us to discover the real source. David wrote, "You have let me experience the joys of life and the exquisite pleasures of your own eternal presence." (Ps. 16:11) Under what circumstances do you think David learned to experience real joy and the exquisite pleasure of God's presence? Was it perhaps when he was hiding in a cave, pursued by Saul, who tried to kill him?

Paul and Silas behaved as if they were experiencing the joys of life when they were in a jail cell, their backs bleeding and their feet in stocks, and yet they were singing praises to

God. (Acts 16:22-25) Richard Wurmbrandt, who suffered for years in a communist prison in Eastern Europe, tells that he discovered the joy of God's presence while he was being tortured in his cell. Christian prisoners in Vietnam report the same phenomenon; it was in the darkest dungeon that they discovered real joy in the presence of God. Daily we get letters from prisoners in this country who say that it was in their blackest moments that God's light broke through to them.

We human beings are creatures of comfort, and who do you think encourages us to believe we can best learn to experience God's presence when everything is going exactly the way we want it? In pleasant circumstances we usually focus our attention on things or people we enjoy, not on God. It is when things are difficult that we can learn to look away from the circumstances and discover the deeper joy there is in being with God.

It is in sickness we can best learn that God can heal us. It is in poverty we can discover how He meets our needs. It is in sorrow we can learn that He comforts us. But we won't learn anything if we decide to focus our attention on our problems. We will only get poorer, sicker, and sadder.

Not long ago I heard a father say to a young man who was courting his daughter, "I want you to treat my daughter every moment as if I were right there." If that is what an earthly father wants for his daughter, what do you think our Heavenly Father wants for us? He is with us every moment, and He wants us to act as if we believe it. Your feelings may tell you that you are lonely, but God's Word says He is with you. Which will you believe? If you aren't sure, you need to repent once more of double-mindedness and look to Jesus. Each time you do, your faith will grow and His presence and His joy will become more and more real to you.

When we make up our minds to believe that God uses problems and pain to bring us a deeper joy in His presence, we are able to be truly glad when the problems come. We can choose to surrender our old feelings to God and focus our full attention on Christ in joyful praise.

Some religious cults teach that our body and natural instincts are evil and must be ignored or denied. That is a twisting of what God tells us in His Word. He created our bodies and gave us instincts and feelings. When we surrender it all to Him, it is like a seed that falls into the ground and emerges as a beautiful new plant. Our physical body and our feelings, fully surrendered to God, will take on new life, even while we are still on this earth. We will enjoy a real measure of greater health and vigor, and our feelings will become part of the experience of our new joy in Christ.

When we choose to shift our allegiance from our feelings to the Holy Spirit, our old, demanding nature is put to death. The new you is able to experience the exquisite pleasures of God's presence in a way that involves your physical, emotional and spiritual being.

Next to our bodies, our concept of time causes the biggest stumbling block to faith for many of us. We live in a natural world where events are measured in chronological order, and we project our time-concept to our relationship with an eternal God.

God created time. He uses it, but He is not limited by it. "But you should never lose sight of this fact, dear friends, that time is not the same with the Lord as it is with us — to Him a day may be a thousand years, and a thousand years only a day." (II Pet. 3:8 Phillips)

There is no past or future with God, only an on-going NOW. Jesus told the puzzled Jews, "I tell you in solemn truth, before there was an Abraham, I AM!" (Jn. 8:58 Phillips) If we suddenly lifted the time dimension we are used to, we would see Jesus hanging on the cross for our sins right NOW. We would also see Him risen from the grave right NOW.

To measure God's answer to our prayers by the time it takes for us to *see* results is like trying to measure weight by the calendar. The clock or the calendar is totally unreliable for that purpose, so we might as well shift our attention to something more trustworthy. God's Word says, "And this is the confidence that we have in Him, that, if we ask any thing according to His will, He heareth us: and if we know that He hear us, whatsoever we ask, we know that we have granted us as our *present possessions* the requests made of Him." (I Jn 5:14,15 KJV & Amp)

In God's dimension we already *have* the answer. You may say, "But that isn't *my* understanding of time; it doesn't help me right this minute! If you are a Christian, you have already entered God's dimension of eternity — His eternal NOW. "I have written like this to you who already believe in the name of God's Son so that you may be quite sure that, here and now, you possess eternal life." (I John 5:13 Phillips) It is our double-mindedness that causes us to look out of the corner of our eye at this world's clocks and calendars while we try to muster enough faith to believe that God will answer our prayer some day. That will never work. We have the power to decide which time-plan we want to follow — God's, or our old one.

David discovered how it worked. He wrote, ". . . My times are in Your hands. . . ." (Ps. 31:15) The Holy Spirit tells you that is true for you as well, but the old you, still bound to this physical world and its time-table, will say, "Look, it's been six months now and God hasn't answered my prayer. He probably never will."

We can be a slave of time, or allow God to teach us how to use the time He gives us. Then we'll never have to worry about having too much or too little time. God gives us exactly the time we need to do what He wants us to do. Do you feel too young — or that you're growing old too fast? Are you bored or always hurried? Surrender your time to God. Confess your double-mindedness. He forgives you and gladly takes over the management of your days.

If you are waiting for an answer to prayer, you are looking in the wrong direction, and are letting the passing hours and days weaken your faith. Instead, you can choose to let each

passing minute strengthen your faith. Fasten your eyes on
Jesus; remind yourself that in God's dimension of time all
prayers are answered already. Then be happy for the opportunity to exercise your faith. A weight-lifter holds his weights a
little longer each day, and grows stronger muscles. With each
second, minute, hour, or day, we hold on to our decision to
believe God no matter what earthly clocks may say, our faith
grows. We are practicing believing something we haven't seen
yet, and as our faith grows, our heart becomes more and more
united and our vision becomes more and more single-minded.
And we come closer to oneness with the Father.

I used to be extremely irritated when people were late for
appointments. I would get headaches and stomach-aches because these people didn't understand — as I understood — how
precious time is. They thought nothing of wasting it!

Once I was scheduled to be on a TV program. Another
minister was to have the first half of the program, and I was to
be interviewed next. I had a lot of important things I wanted to
say, and waited with one eye on the clock for the other fellow to
finish. But when his time was up, he went right on talking. The
interviewer tried, but couldn't stop him. I thought, "Lord, this
is a disgrace! He is wasting *my* time. Why don't you shut him
up so we can get on with something more important!"

When the man finally quit, there were only a few minutes
left. I must confess my prayer was not completely wholehearted when I said, "Lord, You could have shut up that
windbag any time You wanted. Since You didn't, You must
have a reason for letting me sit here and wait. Thank You for
the whole episode. Forgive me for criticizing the other man —
and thank You for what You're going to do with the few
minutes we've got left."

There was no time for involved explanations. I launched
right into challenging the viewers to thank God for their
problems instead of complaining about them, and He would
respond in ways that would amaze them. I encouraged parents
to praise God for run-away children, wives for missing hus-

bands, the sick to rejoice in their illnesses, and those who had financial difficulties to be glad for their unpaid bills.

Within minutes the network phones started ringing. The response from listeners was so unusual that the interviewer was notified by the station manager to keep the program on the air past the regular schedule. The stories kept coming in as more viewers reported amazing results to their prayers of praise. A mother thanked God for her son who had been missing for six months. In a few minutes there was a knock on her door. Outside stood the son, asking if he could come back home. A wife gave thanks for an alcoholic husband. He interrupted her TV viewing to tell her that for the first time in ten years the thought of alcohol made him ill.

I had thought God's message could be held back by a 'lack of time.' I forgot that He is the owner of all time. He can make the sun go forward or backward (and He has done it in recorded history). If there isn't enough time, He can create more. How ridiculous for me, His child, to be worried when He can take a day and make it into a thousand years.

My attention had not been fixed on Jesus while I waited for "my turn." Instead, I let my old concept of time convince me that God was not in charge of the situation. I had to confess my sin of double-mindedness and thank Him for His endless patience and mercy. But I could have saved myself a nervous stomach if I had kept my mind where I should have.

Our mind is our control center. That is where we register the impulses from our senses and our emotions. That is where our understanding measures new impressions against our feelings and our stored-up knowledge, and we make our decision how to act or respond to a situation.

Satan likes to appeal to our understanding. He puts such clever thoughts in our minds that it makes us proud to think them. He encourages us to rationalize our own behavior and thoughts, and to question anything the Holy Spirit tells us. Always his goal is to divert our attention from God. Once he accomplishes that, he knows we'll slide quickly downhill into the trap he has for us.

I was wondering how best to illustrate this point in a sermon, and thought to myself, "Here I am trying to find out what God wants me to say on the subject — but I'm sure Satan is trying to get my attention, too. What could he be saying?" Right away, the thought came, "I'm probably not working on the right message!" I turned that over in my mind for awhile. It was probably true. I didn't know *what* to say. If it was the right message, God would have given me some ideas, wouldn't he?

I said out loud to myself, "I'm going to trust the Lord to give me the right words . . ." But even as I said it, I was thinking, "I must not be trusting the Lord enough for Him to show me what to say — or I would know something by now . . . besides, even if I could say anything worthwhile on the subject, people probably wouldn't understand me!" I sat there thinking until I became so discouraged I put down the pen and muttered, "There's no use in even trying. If I do my best, it won't be good enough anyway!"

Where was my attention focused? Not on Jesus, but on the thoughts stirred up in my mind by Satan. He will rob us and cheat us and take away all our peace and joy and faith if we let him — but *only* if we let him.

Maybe you don't believe that Satan can do that. You are a rational, intelligent human being and no one can invade your mind, you think. But do you know that Satan's most clever lie is to tell you that he does not even exist, or that he does not speak in your thoughts? We are proud of our understanding, and no one knows that better than the devil. That is why he makes his arguments so reasonable and logical, appealing to our pride in our intellect. God's Word warns us, "Trust in the Lord with all thine heart; and lean not unto thine own understanding." (Prov. 3:5 KJV)

I am so glad for the things God has given me to understand, but if I allow my understanding to keep me from believing what God says, then I am using my understanding in the wrong way. People often come to me with a Bible verse they don't understand, and sometimes I have to tell them I don't understand it either. At one time or another we all say, "I wish I understood why God is doing what He is doing," or, "If I could only understand what that means."

I can focus on the things I don't understand in the Bible and soon be completely confused. How much better it is to focus on what I *do* understand. It is easy for me today to understand that God loves me and wants me to be grateful for everything He does in my life. Just thinking about that makes me rejoice. But I am aware of Satan whispering in my thoughts now and then, "Merlin, don't you think you ought to worry about all the things you *don't* understand? After all, you are a pastor, and people come to you for answers." That sounds pretty sensible, doesn't it, but I know from experience where it will get me.

Now when I come across a difficult passage in the Bible, I look to Jesus and follow the Holy Spirit's advice: "If any of you lack wisdom, let him ask of God — and it shall be given him." Only the Holy Spirit can open our eyes to the things God wants us to understand. If the passage still puzzles me, I can decide to concentrate on what I am certain of: God loves me, and if He wanted me to understand, I would. Therefore I can safely trust the things I don't know to my Heavenly Father, who understands everything.

Our understanding falls into the same category as the rest of our old nature. When we try to use it on our own, it traps us in double-mindedness and confusion. When we surrender it, God will use it to His purpose, and we will discover that He lets us understand things we could never figure out on our own.

Why is it that some people are filled with joy and gladness, while others are gloomy and depressed? So often I have observed two people in identical circumstances. Both have been diagnosed as having terminal cancer. Or both have been fired from their jobs. Or they have lost a close relative in death. Or their wives want divorces. One is miserable, but the other radiates joy. What is it? It is because one has learned to center his attention on Jesus; the other looks at the problem.

Try an experiment. Let one object near you represent Jesus Christ. Pick another object to the left or right to represent everything that you think is wrong with your life. Look at that second object for awhile and think about all the things you wish were happening that aren't. Think of every problem, every difficult person, every pain. Just let your mind dwell on those things for a minute or two. You feel utterly miserable, don't you?

Now look at the object representing Jesus. He loves you. He has overcome every problem you can imagine. He has forgiven every sin of which you are guilty. He put every thing and every person into your life to show you His love. He has come to fill you with joy and peace. Doesn't that make you feel better? Even if you don't *feel* better yet, can you see that things *are* better from this perspective?

Jesus came into this world to tell us that He would do for us the things we can't do for ourselves. We can't erase our problems and our pains by ignoring them, but there is something we *can* do. Maybe right now you feel so weakened by your disease, so depressed by your problem, so misused and misunderstood and abused by people that you feel you can't do anything. God knows how weak and low you are. He knows you can't pick yourself up. But He wants you to do the one thing He has given you the ability to do. Open your eyes and look at Him. ". . . If there is anything worthy of praise, think on and weigh and take account of these things — fix your minds on them." (Phil. 4:8 b. Amp) Think of Jesus. Is He worthy of praise? Let your mind dwell on who He is and what he has done until the darkness around you gives way to light.

If you see someone walking down the street, his face radiant and filled with joy, don't assume he doesn't have any problems. He may have ten times more problems than you ever had. Do you say, "Why can't I be like that? Why am I so miserable and he so happy?" You know the answer. He has learned to fix his attention on Christ. He has learned how to bring Heaven into Hell.

You have the ability to do the same. If a problem comes, you can say, "Praise God, it isn't my problem; it is His. My attention is over here on Jesus, who tells me 'Let not your heart be troubled; ye believe in God, believe also in me' " (Jn 14:1 KJV)

Satan is whispering from the sidelines, reminding you to worry, and telling you that no matter what you do, it will be wrong.

He is a liar. Nothing will be wrong — everything will be right if you decide to keep on looking at Jesus with a single eye and a united heart. Fix your thoughts on Him. Repent of all double-mindedness, and you can say with David, "My heart is fixed, O God; My heart is steadfast and confident! I will sing and make melody . . . I will praise and give thanks . . ." (Ps. 57:7,9 Amp)

## 8. Authority – Submission

The day I got out of the army after over two years of service in World War II, I actually jumped up and down for joy. It wasn't the joy of the Lord — no, I was just so glad to be out of "that rotten, stinking Army." I hated to be told when to get up and what to wear and what to do and how to do it every minute of the day. I was so glad to get out I declared I would never even turn and look at the Army as long as I lived.

Then one day after I had finished my education in seminary and was ready to serve God, I said, "Here I am, Lord, what do you want me to do?"

"Go back into the Army as a chaplain!"

It took me a long time to swallow that, but I finally decided I must go back in for three years. There were things I liked about the Army, but I couldn't stand to take orders from anybody, and once I was back in, I realized it was worse than I remembered. Now I was an officer and a chaplain, and I still had to get up when they told me, wear what they wanted me to wear, fold my blankets exactly the way they said, and eat what they served me. Sometimes they said, "Get up at four o'clock, fall out at five, march until six-thirty, lay out your full field pack, stand there and wait for inspection." I had to do push ups and crawl through the mud with the troops. It was disgusting and annoying, but now that I was a chaplain I not only had to do it, but act as if *I enjoyed it* in front of the men!

The end of three years came, and I thought, "Praise the Lord, I'm getting out." But the Lord made it very clear, "Merlin, I think you need a little more." So I stayed in another year, then five and six, and finally twenty; and as the time went on, something began to happen inside me. I was learning more about God's love and why He puts us in hard places. The rebellion in me died down, and after a while I actually enjoyed following orders. I had learned a submissiveness of spirit that had never before been a part of me, and God knew that without that submissiveness I would never be able to experience as fully His love and His plan for my life.

There are some things in Christianity that are harder to understand and more difficult to accept than other things. Submission is one of them. When we become Christians, one of the first things we are told about our new life is that, "But as many as received Him, (Christ), to them gave He the power to become the sons of God." (Jn. 1:12 KJV) When I first discovered that verse I thought, "Wonderful, all that power is mine!" Then I found even better news: "And if children, then heirs; heirs of God, and joint-heirs with Christ; . . ." (Rom. 8:17 KJV) Just imagine being joint-heirs with the Son of God, who said, ". . . All power is given unto me in heaven and in earth." (Matt. 28:18)

That's just great! But something puzzled me, and maybe puzzles you. If all that power is yours, how come you can't do anything with it? Jesus had authority over the wind and the weather. He could still a storm, but when did you last still a storm? Jesus had authority over the water. He could decide to walk on it — or go down into it to be baptized. I haven't been able to make that choice for myself yet.

Here is where submission fits into the picture. Our authority in Christ is only valid when we submit to Him, and here is the other side of the same coin — submission isn't real, until we understand our authority as children of God!

If that sounds confusing, it is because we start out with a completely wrong concept of authority and submission. In the

process of growing up, some of us have learned how to get our
own way always. We have learned to demand and manipulate
and take control over people and situations. We call that
authority. Others among us grew up learning that we could
never have our own way. We were too weak to stand up to those
who pushed us around or took advantage of us. We call that
submission.

Between those two extremes are the rest of us, who have
developed schemes to get our way sometimes, and have felt
that we've been forced to give in to people or circumstances the
rest of the times. Starting with our parents, brothers and
sisters, bullies, we feel we've been squeezed and pressed to our
limit. When God says, "Submit!" we don't like it.

In recent years we've seen scores of "liberation" movements
pop up. They all teach that we have "rights" as human beings
and need to stand up for ourselves. But these movements are
all based on the same false concept of authority and submission. They tell us that authority means to take what's "right-
fully" yours, and submission means to let everybody walk all
over you.

We need to understand that these ideas of authority and
submission are counterfeits of the real thing. When we try to
apply them in our Christian life it doesn't work.

True authority is a legal and rightful power given us to
command or act. It isn't something we claim for ourselves. True
submission is the voluntary act of committing ourselves to the
will of someone else. It isn't something forced on us.

In the Christian life, authority and submission depend on
each other. Neither "works" without the other. Jesus showed
us the principle in action. He said, "For I have not spoken of
myself; but the Father which sent me, he gave me a commandment, what I should say, and what I should speak." (Jn
12:49 KJV)

Jesus, who had been given the rightful power to command
or act, spoke words of authority only when His Father told Him
what to say. The Son, who had all authority, voluntarily

committed himself to the will of the Father. He said, "I can of mine own self do nothing; . . . I seek not mine own will, but the will of the Father which hath sent me. (Jn. 5:30 KJV)

The most powerful thing that Jesus Christ ever did, was when He broke Satan's hold over this world. Did He do it by exercising all His authority? No, He submitted. The tremendous power behind the crucifixion was the perfect submission of Christ. He could have slain His accusers with a word or by calling ten thousand angels, but then there would have been no redemption for a lost world — no victory over evil. You and I are free today because Jesus submitted to death in our place.

There would have been no power behind that event if Jesus had not held the authority to save Himself. He said, "No one can kill me without my consent — I lay down my life voluntarily. For I have the right and power to lay it down when I want to and also the right and power to take it again. For the Father has given me this right." (Jn 10:18)

The submission God requires from us is always a voluntary act of obedience. When we do it, God responds by releasing His power and His authority into our situation. Involuntary submission releases no such power, and only makes us more miserable.

An army commander wants to be surrounded by men who can submit to orders; not out of fear, because then they would be cowardly soldiers, but gladly, because they trust the judgment of their commander and know that obedience is necessary if their mission is to be successful.

Think of the picture of a well-trained dog. He holds his head up high and his tail is poised. He eagerly obeys the least of his master's commands. There is a beautiful relationship of loyalty and trust between them.

Now think of a dog cowering with his tail between his legs before his cruel master. This dog also obeys, but it is because he fears the whipping he'll get if he doesn't. There is no bond of love and respect between the two, and we know that if the dog got a chance, he would run away.

The dog who eagerly obeys his master because he loves him shows a picture of true submission. God has given us the freedom of choice. Our obedience must be a voluntary thing — but we human beings don't like to submit any more than we like to surrender or repent or forgive. We came into this world screaming and demanding our own way, and submission will always be contrary to our old nature.

When we become Christians, it is hard to surrender that old nature to God. We can only do it a little at a time, because we can't bear to give up all the controls to God at once. When we discover the glorious news that God gives us the right to become His children, we want to shout, "Hooray, I'm free — nobody has any authority over me but God !"

That is right — but what does God tell you to do? He says, "Now I want you to submit — to my Word, to the circumstances in which I have placed you, and to the people with whom I have surrounded you!"

Why do we have to submit? God knows our old nature, and the only way it can be tamed is through obedience. The root of all sin is disobedience and rebellion — and that destroys our relationship with God. Jesus said, "Not every one that saith unto me Lord, Lord, shall enter into the kingdom of heaven; but he that *doeth* the will of my Father which is in heaven." (Matt. 7:21 KJV)

If we refuse to submit to God's will, our Christian life comes to a grinding halt. We can't have oneness with Christ or abide in His love. We will have no peace or joy. "If ye keep my commandments, ye shall abide in my love; . . . these things have I spoken unto you, that my joy might remain in you, and that your joy might be full." (Jn 15:10,11 KJV)

If submission is contrary to our old nature, how do we learn it? First, recognize that the old "submission" — giving in to something you can't control, and resenting it — isn't submission. Ask God to take away the old, rebellious feelings and teach you true submission — the kind that brings oneness with the Father and releases His power and authority into your life.

Jesus submitted willingly because He knew who He was. Here is the key to true submission. We must know who we are. Do you think you are a poor, mistreated human being, pressed by circumstances, and forgotten by God? Then you are in no position to truly submit. You need to know deep down in your heart that you are a child of God — with all the rights and privileges He has given you — and that not for a moment do you have reason to doubt His love. Now you can submit without fear. The only true foundation for submission is to be absolutely sure of our Heavenly Father's love.

A small child is required to obey his parents and has no real choice in the matter. Then comes the moment when he finds out he doesn't *have* to obey. He is strong enough to resist. Have you ever observed a teenager struggling to discover who he is and what his rights and responsibilities are as a person? During the process he often lashes out against all authority, arguing with his parents, and standing up for his "rights."

If the teenager doesn't know, deep down in his heart, that his parents love him, resentment and a sense of rejection can boil into serious, open rebellion. Thousands of young people are caught in that trap today. The teenager or young adult who comes through the crisis into maturity and true submission is the one who knows that he is loved, and that his parents only want the best for him.

As Christians we face a parallel crisis as we struggle to find our true identity in Christ. The way to true maturity leads through submission, but we can't get there unless we know our Heavenly Father really loves us and only wants the best for us. That knowledge is the anchor that keeps us through the storm while our old, stubborn ego battles against the difficult circumstances to which God asks us to submit.

If you doubt His love, stop right now and go back over a few basic truths God tells us in His Word. You are His child if you have decided to believe. You are loved, because God sent Jesus to die for you. Pin some of your favorite scripture verses on your wall where you are reminded of them often. Fasten your thoughts on them. Repeat them out loud to yourself. Are you going to believe who God says you are, or pay attention to your doubts?

When you know who you are, submission is no threat to your true identity, but it spells doom for your old nature, and that is why the old you fights it so hard. At first, even submitting in little things is a battle. Tell God you are willing and confess your feelings of rebellion. As you submit, you will find that God changes you inside. It is a life-long process, but the beginning is the hardest. For each step you take, it will get easier.

In the army, it is the soldier who submits eagerly who is noticed by his superiors and is first promoted from his rank. With each promotion, the soldier finds that the outward demands for submission become less, while his voluntary allegiance and obedience become more and more a part of him. It is the same way in the Christian life. At first we find ourselves pressed by circumstances and difficult people on all sides. But as we submit, and God begins to work that submission into our hearts, we experience a new oneness with Christ. Now we find that true submission takes the sting out of painful circumstances and relationships. We can actually enjoy them, just as I finally learned to enjoy taking orders in the army.

When first we begin to submit, we reluctantly say, "God, I'll accept your will for me, but I would prefer it my own way." We still do most of the deciding and only allow Christ to be a part-time consultant. Next we are able to say, "I admit you seem to know better how to run my life; I'll be glad to follow your directions whenever I get fouled up myself." We give Jesus perhaps half the controls over our life. But when we can say, "Lord, I want to do only your will and none of mine," we are coming closer to the maturity God wants for us.

Paul wrote to the Christians in Colossae, ". . . We want to be able to present each one (of the believers) to God, perfect, because of what Christ has done for each of them." (Col. 1:28) What is Christian perfection? That is when someone looks at you and sees only Christ. There is only one way God can make that transformation in you and me, and that is through our submission.

When we know we are God's children, loved by Him, we also know that He has given us authority over our old, rebellious nature. We can decide to submit voluntarily and gladly to whatever difficult circumstances God has given us. That kind of submission is a powerful thing. It not only transforms us, but releases God's power and authority into our surroundings. The more we submit, the more His power is released.

Suffering is never meant to be the end for God's children. Satan will tell you that submitting to suffering means you'll always have to suffer. The very opposite is true. You may be in a prison cell facing 25 years, or on a hospital bed with painful months ahead of you. Perhaps financial or personal problems are mounting up, threatening to crush you. Satan whispers that you are a victim of circumstances, but he is a liar. You can exercise your authority as a beloved child of God by voluntarily submitting to those circumstances, and thanking God for them. Now the power of evil has been broken. You and your situation are safe in God's hands, and He is in perfect control. You know it is true, because your inner turmoil has been replaced by His peace.

We often quote the verse in the Bible that says we are joint heirs with Christ — but we seldom pay attention to the second part of the statement that we are ". . . joint-heirs with Christ; *if* so be that we suffer with Him, that we may be also glorified together." (Rom. 8:17 KJV)

We are joint heirs with Christ when we joyfully accept suffering with Him. Now can you be glad for every opportunity to submit to a difficulty? You can be sure it will lead to something glorious in your relationship with God.

## 9. Are You Really Glad?

Is there anyone you would rather be or anything you would rather do than be who you are and do what you do right now? Can you think of any change you would like to see in your circumstances?

If the answer is yes, you haven't learned how to be really glad yet.

I know a woman who was born with only one finger on each hand and one toe on each foot. She believed God had made her that way because He wanted to, and she thought He knew what was best for her, so she was grateful. When she was dating her husband-to-be, he came to her house for dinner and she was on her best behavior to impress him. It so happened that she dropped a dish. Can you imagine the thoughts that rushed into her head? But quickly she quipped, "I would say I am all thumbs, but I don't qualify!" There was no embarrassment, only happy laughter.

Later, when they were married, she became the mother of two children. Both were born with only one finger on each hand and one toe on each foot. From the time they were infants, the children were told that they were very special in God's eyes. When the youngest was four years old, he once said to a saleswoman in a store, "I guess you wonder why we only have one finger on our hands. God made us this way for a reason."

Do you believe God made you the way you are for a reason? And put you where you are because He wants you there? Stop and think about it. If you are like me and everybody else I know, you are surrounded by many kinds of circumstances, and you are reacting to them in one of two ways. If you are unhappy about them, they are getting you down. If you are glad, they are lifting you up. So are you going up or down right now?

As children of God we can have authority over our circumstances. How do we use it? By going up, of course — but what is the way up? Think of yourself standing in the surf with the water up to your armpits — and here comes a big wave. If you don't know much about waves, you may try to run from it, but it will suck you back and throw you down with thundering force. Helplessly you tumble around, until, gasping and fighting for breath, you emerge in shallow water, bruised and dripping like a drowning kitten.

Experienced swimmers know a better way. Calmly they face the threatening wave — and dive directly under the foaming crest. Seconds later they emerge on the surface, turn and float easily on the smooth back of the crested wave all the way back to shore.

For a swimmer, the way to be lifted on top of a wave is to dive under it! For a Christian, the way to be lifted on top of a problem is to submit to it.

Most of us know only too well what it means to go down under problems. We've been tossed around, bruised and hurt by circumstances all our lives. But that is not submission. It is exactly the opposite, and the correct word for it is to succumb, which means to sink down, be overcome.

Submission, on the other hand, is that voluntary act of the child of God who knows that his Father is in charge, and who trusts himself in his Father's hands. Submission releases God's authority to overcome the situation.

When we succumb, our eyes are on the problem and our minds are full of complaints. When we submit, our eyes are on Christ, and our minds are full of praise. As time goes on our succumbing will draw us farther and farther down into misery and grief. In contrast, submission will in time lift us into joy and gladness in Christ, even if the problem remains.

Several nations have developed a poisonous gas for use in warfare. It is completely invisible and odorless and the victims breathe it without knowing it is there. Satan has a deadly "gas" that can flow into our hearts and minds while we don't even know what is happening. It is the attitude of complaining. Some of us are so used to complaining that we think it is our natural right, yet it was complaining and murmuring that caused the Israelites to die in the wilderness. Paul warned the early Christians, "And don't murmur against God and his dealings with you, as some of them did, for that is why God sent his Angel to destroy them." (I Cor. 10:10)

Complaining is a deadly sin because it is an expression of disbelief and distrust. You wouldn't complain if you really thought God was in charge and doing what is best for you. When you complain, you succumb. You are being dragged down by your problem, not lifted up.

But if complaining is like an invisible gas, how do we detect it in ourselves? We may be bravely enduring our pain, even saying, "Praise the Lord for it all." Could there still be an attitude of complaining hiding somewhere in us?

Moses warned the Israelites that God's curse would come upon them: "Because thou servedst not the Lord thy God with joyfulness, and with gladness of heart . . ." (Deut. 28:47 KJV) Here is our complaint-detector. ARE YOU REALLY GLAD, DEEP DOWN IN YOUR HEART? Are you glad you have the problem? Glad you hurt? When you're glad, you're not complaining. When you're glad, it means you are sure you are a child of God. You are sure of His love for you and that He is working everything in your life together for your good in a perfect plan. You have reason to be glad because you know that your problem or your pain is there to do you some good. Gladness is a sign of submission.

When we submit to the point of saying, "I am really glad," our praise becomes pure and wholehearted. The next time you want to say, "Praise the Lord," try saying instead, "Lord, I am so glad you let that happen right now!" If your heart isn't in it, then you are hiding a small complaint or unbelief somewhere. One little complaint will keep you from real submission and real praise in that area of your life.

When my last book, *Walking and Leaping*, was published, I was annoyed to discover several printing errors. I remembered to praise the Lord for the mistakes, but I also wrote a letter to the publisher pointing them out, and I know I wasn't able to be glad they happened. It wasn't till I received an answer from the publisher that I discovered how wrong my reaction had been.

The editor wrote, "You might be interested to hear of a letter we received from a lady who was having trouble with some peach trees in her garden. She was reading your book and came across the most notable printing error: "the *peace* that passes understanding" was spelled, "the *peach* that passes understanding." She read this mistake with great rejoicing, seeing in it evidence that God cared for her peach trees. What could we say? Praise the Lord!"

I had let that little problem annoy me and overcome me, and my words of praise had not brought real joy. The complaint hidden in my heart had been unmasked by my lack of gladness, but I had not heeded the warning.

When we learn to submit so completely that gladness and praise fill our hearts continually, we will be lifted above our problems to a new level of life with Christ. Have you ever had a pair of shoes that always hurts your feet, and then gotten a new pair that fits just perfectly? Didn't it feel good? Exchanging a lifelong habit of complaining for one of gladness and praise is just like that.

Does this mean that we are always to submit to every circumstance, both good and evil? What about our authority as God's children? Don't we get to use it sometimes?

There is only one area where God tells us never to submit and always to use our authority — and that is over our sin. Every trial and pain we face is in some way connected with our old sinful nature. But even in this battle, submission comes before authority. "Submit yourselves therefore to God. Resist the devil, and he will flee from you." (James 4:7 KJV) Step one is always submission — that releases our authority to resist evil. But remember that our authority rests solely on God's power. We fight a losing battle in our own strength.

So if you are faced with a small problem — or big ones piled up until you think you can take no more, the first step is to dive straight into it by submitting yourself to God who has control over it all. Ask yourself the complaint-detecting question: "Am I *really* glad everything is the way it is?" If you aren't glad, now is the time to use your authority. Your complaint is a mask for the sin of unbelief and rebellion. Don't let it pull you down into further misery. Resist it by confessing it to God. Be specific and as honest as you can. Tell God you're sorry for not being glad for the way He is handling your life. When you have honestly repented, you know He has forgiven you. Now you can tell Him that you willingly submit to what He has put into your life. When your submission is complete, it brings God's power into your circumstances and gladness into your heart.

David knew what it was to submit and repent. He wrote, "Hear, O Lord, and have mercy upon me: Lord, be thou my helper. Thou hast turned for me my mourning into dancing: thou hast put off my sackcloth, and girded me with gladness;" (Ps. 30:10-11 KJV)

When we submit to God's will and resist evil, He pours gladness over us. "Thou hast loved righteousness, and hated iniquity; therefore God, even thy God, hath anointed thee with the oil of gladness . . ." (Heb. 1:9 KJV)

The sign of wholehearted submission is gladness. That is why David wrote, "Serve the Lord with gladness: come before his presence with singing." (Ps 100:2 KJV) We can't serve God unless we are submitted to His will — and if we aren't glad, then we aren't submitted.

God wants us to serve Him. He has a wonderful plan for you and for me — but how can He guide us in the right direction if we always want our own way? "He leads the humble in what is right, and the humble He teaches His way." (Ps. 25:9 Amp) The humble are those who have learned to submit with gladness to God's will. There is no better place to learn than in difficult circumstances that rub against our natural inclinations.

We say, "Lord, use me. Send me on a great mission. I'll obey Your least command!" Here is what God says to that kind of request: "I already put you on a mission — right where you are. Show me how obedient you are by being really glad for every detail of your circumstances."

I have known young people who were bored at home and in their job, and so they said, "The Lord has called me to spread the gospel and live on faith." They quit their boring job and moved away from their cranky relatives to a distant community where they expect other Christians to give them a place to sleep and food to eat.

That was no act of submission to God's will. Paul gave new Christians some practical advice: "My brothers, let every one of us continue to live his life with God in the state in which he was when he was called." (I Cor. 7:24 Phillips) Paul himself continued in his trade as a tentmaker and supported himself wherever he went to spread the gospel.

God may have called you to do something different from what you are doing now. But if you don't like where you are, you aren't ready to leave yet. Submission to your present circumstances comes first. God has you where you are for a purpose that can only be accomplished when you are completely submitted. The sign of submission is gladness. When you are glad you are there, God may call you to leave — but not before. If you leave on your own, you are headed for bigger problems than the ones you are faced with today.

The same holds true for every other kind of trial with which you may be faced. God means it for good, but the good can't happen until you submit. When you can say, "Thank you, Lord, for the thing that hurts. I am glad it hurts" — then it may go away. But your gladness has taken the sting from the pain, and you know you'll stay glad even if it doesn't go away. The good has been accomplished. Your submission gave you authority over that trial, and God lifted you up above it where you can ride on it safely to wherever God has planned.

We have been conditioned to think of submission as a sign of weakness, but it is the key to our strength. Each problem and pain is designed to help us grow in that strength. As long as a baby lies flat in his crib, he doesn't need much strength. But when he first stands up, he experiences the forces of gravity pulling him down. To walk and run he needs to develop strength. The stronger he gets, the better he can run and jump, but without the downward pull of gravity he would never develop his muscles in the first place.

The early Christians had to contend against powerful forces; persecutions and trials worse than most of us can comprehend. They were forced to leave their homes, were hunted like animals, tortured, thrown to the lions — survived in caves and catacombs. They had little food, water and comforts as we know them. But it was in these circumstances that God taught His people the true source of their strength and joy. It was there they learned to praise Him with hearts of gladness.

If you are glad and thankful only when things go your way, you are like a baby lying in a crib. You haven't begun to rely on God's strength against the downward pull of your problems yet. So often we first think of getting God's help when a major tragedy comes into our life. Trying to Praise Him for a big problem can be a discouraging experience, because we have a lifetime habit of reacting to every disappointment by complaining.

Like the baby learning to walk, we can best start by exercising our spiritual muscles on small problems. Each time we are able to respond the right way we find ourselves lifted up and ready to face a bigger problem with increasing confidence. Take something minor, like the wave of irritation you feel when another driver pulls ahead of you into the last parking place on the block. Are you going to let that wave pull you under or lift you up?

Stop right there and take authority over your irritation. Confess it as a sinful complaint. Tell God you're sorry you aren't glad, but you are willing to be. Then thank Him for letting that other driver park ahead of you. He must have a better parking space waiting. Aren't you glad you didn't get the one you wanted?

Have you ever complained when you bought something that turned out to be defective and the store refused to refund your money? I have, and as long as I was mad that thing churned inside me and poisoned everything I did and thought for days. I was being pulled down fast. Remember that you are a child of God with all the power and authority He gives you. No one can take advantage of you. If it seems to you that they are doing it, you are forgetting that God is in complete control of every store and sales manager in the world. If He allows them to keep your money or charge you too much, it must be because you need that experience. You can be glad it happened!

If minor irritations cause you to complain, how will you be able to stand in a real battle against evil? Everything that happens to you is brought by God for a good purpose. Submission lifts us above it and releases God's strength and joy. Satan encourages us to complain, because he knows that the more we complain, the longer we suffer.

I received a letter from a teenage girl who told me that her father had recently died. He had been a Christian for only three months, but the girl was grateful. "My parents were divorced and I lived with my father," she wrote. "My mother isn't a Christian yet, but now she has come to live with us. I know that is why Jesus took my dad home with Him. We are praying for my mom and we know God loves her so much."

That girl did not sink under with grief. She submitted to the circumstances and was glad because she knew God was in charge. The more severe the downward pull is in our lives, the greater is the opportunity for our spiritual muscles to grow. Paul wrote, "I can do all things through Christ which strengtheneth me." (Phil 4:13 KJV) Paul had discovered the truth of that statement through some very difficult circumstances.

Our strength is not our own, it is Christ. We experience it first when we surrender to Him, but it is through our daily submission that His authority and His strength take control in our lives.

Another passage in the Bible tells us that, ". . . The joy of the Lord is your strength." (Neh. 8:10 KJV) It is a joy that can only come through complete submission. When we rely completely on God and say, "I am glad everything is the way it is!" His strength lifts us up and transforms every problem, every pain into joy.

That kind of joy and strength never comes to the proud; only to the humble. The proud person does not know how to submit himself to God and can never experience oneness with Him. "Therefore anyone who humbles himself as this little child, is the greatest in the Kingdom of Heaven," Jesus told his followers. (Matt. 18:4)

The purpose of submission is to reduce our old selves so that Christ can increase in our lives — less of us and more of Him.

I had a letter from a young assistant pastor who told of his joy in praising God for everything. It was the tone of the letter that impressed me. The source of that young man's joy was that he was convinced of his own insignificance and God's greatness. "God has shown me in so many ways what a nothing I really am, and I praise Him because now I understand better how great He is. It is the greatest feeling in the world to know that God loves me. I feel very small and not very wise, but I and all my problems are right in the palm of God's hand. I worry about nothing any more. God has everything under control. Praise Him!"

Are you worried about anything? Do you sometimes stay awake at night fearing a phone call with bad tidings? Are you afraid you will lose your job? Or come down with cancer? So many people live with fears. Why? We only fear those things we have not yet submitted to God.

"Praise the Lord! For all who fear God and trust in him are blessed beyond expression. Yes, happy is the man who delights in doing his commands . . . Such a man will not be overthrown by evil circumstances . . . He does not fear bad news, nor live in dread of what may happen. For he is settled in his mind that Jehovah will take care of him." (Ps 112:1,6,7) He is settled in his mind.

I am convinced that we will experience some very difficult times ahead — economic hardships, collapse of law and order, shortages of food — frightening things if you haven't learned to depend on God's strength through submission.

Fear pumps adrenalin into the body and gets us moving. It gives us unusual strength to do things we cannot normally do. Think of the effect faith could have on our body if we allowed it to take instant control over us the way we have let fear do in the past — faith that causes us to submit to God without a moment's hesitation. Think of the tremendous power of God released through our submission!

Is it so hard to understand why God wants us to submit to His will? He knows what will happen in our lives when we stop complaining and learn to say, "Lord, I'm really glad!"

## 10. Who Is Number One?

Do you think it would be easier to be perfect if you weren't surrounded by difficult people? But wait a minute — why do you think those people are there? We often quote a verse that says, "My God will supply all that you need from His glorious resources in Christ Jesus." (Phil. 4:19 Phillips) Did you ever stop to think that God also supplies the people with whom you need to live?

Maybe you say, "But, Lord, I don't need an alcoholic husband — or an unloving wife — or an unreasonable boss — or a runaway, rebellious child!" If that is what you have, that is what God says you need, or He would not give it to you.

We have talked about how God puts us in difficult circumstances to strip us of our old nature and teach us joyful submission to His will. Nothing teaches us submission as effectively as having to live with difficult people. Often God brings someone into our lives who just irks us to death, because we need that person. That person brings out the worst in us — and we need to see that in ourselves in order to get rid of it. Our stubborn, self-willed ego, bristling, says, "I don't want to do what anybody tells me to do — I won't take that kind of nonsense from anybody!!" Do you recognize that ugly thing inside rearing up, always wanting to have the last word? It is called the flesh, the old nature, and only submission can bring it under control.

Paul gave some specific guidelines for the Christian life:

1. ". . . be filled instead with the Holy Spirit . . .

2. Always give thanks for everything to our God and Father in the name of our Lord Jesus Christ.

3. Honor Christ by submitting to each other.
   (Eph. 5:18,20,21)

Step number three is the hardest for us to accept' — but without it, the other two won't work. Submission to other people is an absolutely necessary part of the Christian growth process. God, who knows us better than we do, gives us opportunities to be in submission to certain people just so that we can become what He wants us to be.

Even Jesus learned submission through experience. As a young boy He had more wisdom and understanding than anyone else in the whole world, and I am sure He was aware of it. When He was twelve, His parents brought Him to the temple in Jerusalem. They returned home, but Jesus remained in deep discussion with the learned Temple teachers, who marveled at His understanding. When the parents discovered that their boy was left behind, they worried and came looking for Him. When they found Him, He was told to come home immediately.

We read that he went home with them to Nazareth and was obedient to them. (See Luke 2:41-52) Think of it, the perfect Son of God lived in total submission to his earthly parents, although He was much wiser than they. He kept His mouth shut and did what He was told. He listened and learned. What did He learn? "And even though Jesus was God's Son, He had to learn from experience what it was like to obey . . ." (Heb. 5:8)

Jesus was thirty years old when He began His ministry. The power behind His authority was His perfect submission to His Heavenly Father and to the circumstances and people among whom His Father put Him.

If you are young and want to have the joy of the Lord — obey your parents! Maybe they are always picking on you.

Maybe they don't trust you. Maybe they don't understand your religion and want you to stop talking about Jesus and stay home from church. You may say, "I'm going to obey God, not man," and go to church anyway. You are making a mistake. God's first instruction to you is: "Children, obey your parents; this is the right thing to do because God has placed them in authority over you." (Eph. 6:1) You will be closer to God when you stay home from church in obedience to your parents than if you go there against their will.

Try being submissive for at least one week — then if you can do it, try another week — and another — and a month — and a year. Can you do it joyfully? Maybe you say, "All I can do is just do it!" That is fine for a starter, but in the meantime look inside yourself and see why you can't do it gladly.

Can you believe that God gave you the parents you have because you need them? If He had wanted it differently, He could have put you in another family. If you are living with foster parents or adoptive parents, the same holds true. God placed them in authority over you because you need it. Can you thank God for them? Are you really glad they are the way they are? If you aren't glad, then you are complaining, and remember, complaining is a serious sin. God will forgive you and give you a new love for your parents when you ask Him for it.

If you love them, submission is easy because love is ". . . never haughty or selfish or rude. Love does not demand its own way. It is not irritable or touchy . . ." (I Cor. 13:5) Does that describe the way you feel and act toward your parents?

A young man wrote me, "My parents are unsaved, and my heart's desire is that they come to know Jesus. I try to be a good Christian, but every time I say or do something against my parents' will, they blame it on Jesus. I get so discouraged and depressed."

The most powerful way to demonstrate Christianity to your parents is to obey them in love. Remember that you are in a three-way relationship. As you submit first to God, He will

help you submit to your parents in such a way that they can see
Christ and His love in you.

God has placed parents in authority over children, but
authority will be false and destructive unless we learn to
combine it with true submission. The first step is to submit to
God's will and recognize that He has given us exactly the
children we need. If they are bright or slow, talented or clumsy,
obedient or unruly, they are what we need — and we are what
they need. God matched us up with infinite care, whether our
children are of our flesh and blood or came to us some other
way.

There is chaos and constant friction in homes across our
land because we as parents have not learned to use our proper
authority and submission. We always want the very best for
our children, and we tend to blame ourselves when they do
wrong. In our frustration we often give up all attempts to
discipline or become too harsh. The Bible tells us there is a
better way: "And now a word to you parents. Don't keep on
scolding and nagging your children, making them angry and
resentful. Rather, bring them up with the loving discipline the
Lord himself approves, with suggestions and godly advice."
(Eph. 6:4)

Don't be too harsh, and don't let them go without loving
discipline. That task is impossible unless we submit to God and
ask Him to meet our children's needs through us. He alone
knows their needs — it may be a spanking, or a fishing trip
with Dad. If we haven't understood our dependency on God
before, we have a chance to discover it when our children are
growing up!

For most of us the problems surface when our children are
teenagers. Parents come to me who cannot understand why
their once loving and affectionate children have become distant, rebellious and even hateful. At this point it is easy for
parents to give in to a sense of guilt. We are afraid we have
failed completely.

From God's perspective, things look different. Our family crisis is a wonderful opportunity for us to learn together. Giving thanks for the problem is the first step.

A common failing among us parents is that we think of our children as belonging to us — we cling to them and try to mold their lives. We need to submit our children to God and realize that their relationship with Him is more important than their relationship with us. Can we thank Him for being in charge of them? Can we thank Him for everything they do and say?

A mother told me how her teenage daughter would get mad and swear at her, yelling, "I hate you!" The mother would yell back, telling her to shut up, but the daily screaming sessions only got longer and louder. At this point the mother came to our church and began learning how to praise God in every situation.

One evening her daughter exploded with a stream of curses, but the mother remained calm and responded with, "Praise the Lord!" The daughter got madder when she couldn't stir up her mother and accused her of drinking. Still the mother kept smiling and saying, "Thank you, God, for all this."

Enraged, the daughter closed herself in her room for the evening. The next morning she came to breakfast a new creature, smiling and sweet. That was three years ago, her mother told me. They haven't had a single argument since.

God's power came through the mother's submission and changed the daughter. But what if God required that you be firm with your teenager? Even then your firmness must be based on submission, asking God to give you the right words to speak in love.

If your eighteen year-old says, "Thanks for the advice, but I choose not to obey," the decision is his. Can you be grateful? Can you submit him to God and rest in the knowledge that the disciplining is now up to his Heavenly Father?

A Christian couple dedicated their daughter to God and raised her in church. When she reached sixteen, she fell in love and ran away. With her boyfriend, she drifted across the country, calling home only to tell her parents that she was happy and did not want their interference.

The parents grieved for three years. Then in a Bible study group they discussed the verse, "And we know that all things work together for good to them that love God, to them who are the called according to His purpose." (Rom. 8:28 KJV) The leader interpreted this to mean they ought to thank God for every circumstance in their lives. His words upset the mother, who thought God did not intend them to be thankful that their daughter was living in sin.

A few weeks later a friend gave them *Prison to Praise*. They read it, but didn't think it applied to them. Next they read *Power in Praise* and studied carefully the scriptures referred to in the book. It finally convinced them that God wanted them to trust Him enough to praise Him, believing that their daughter was doing what she was doing because God allowed it. He was going to use that situation for something good.

Once they submitted to the situation, they found a new peace and joy in their own lives. They were trusting God in a new way, with new authority and power to help others.

At this time their daughter and her boyfriend were living in a dilapidated shack in another state. The girl was searching through some boxes left by the tenants of another shack, when she found a cardboard fan advertising a local funeral parlor. There was a picture of Jesus the Shepherd, holding a lamb. Suddenly the girl found herself thinking, "God loves me like Jesus loves that little lamb." The thought did not go away, and a couple of days later she found a crumpled page torn from a Bible. Hungrily she read the familiar words and realized that she longed to find her way back to God. She called her father and asked him to pray that she would know what to do. His response was, "Honey, you know you can find Jesus right where you are if you only talk to Him."

That week she called home several times and finally told her parents, "I have given my life to God. I want to do His will." She asked her father if she should leave her boyfriend and come home, but her father said, "I'll be glad to send you a plane ticket, but you must make the decision to come when you feel it is the right thing to do."

The daughter loved the man with whom she was living, but finally decided that it was wrong to stay with him. She flew home to a reunion with her parents and filled her days with Bible studies and prayer. Her submission to God's will was so thorough that she matured rapidly in her Christian life.

A few months later her old boyfriend came looking for her. She was not home, but a Christian friend was there. He greeted the young man warmly and asked if he knew Christ.

"No," the fellow shook his head. "I've never been to church, but I know my girl loved me and wouldn't leave unless something important came up. I would like to pray to her God and see if I can find what she has found."

A couple of hours later he accepted Christ as his Savior. He had no job and no material possessions, but stayed with the Christian friend of the family, and soon was an enthusiastic dedicated Christian. He wanted to do God's will, and was willing to give up hope of ever getting his girl back if that was God's plan.

About this time God arranged the circumstances to bring these two back together again. Their wedding was one of the happiest the church had ever seen, and they are active together in Christian work today.

The story has a happy ending, but I know parents of runaway children who cannot submit their children to God, and who cannot resist trying to control the young people when they find them. For lack of submission there is still a painful, broken relationship.

Being a wife or a husband gives us another wonderful opportunity to submit. Aren't you glad your husband is exactly the way he is? Do you appreciate that God picked your wife especially to fill your need? A woman in our church told how she first tried to praise God for her husband, hoping God would change him. But nothing happened. Then she started listening

to the sermons on how to submit to what God wants for us. She
began looking at her own attitudes and asked God to change
her instead. As she was changed, so was her husband.

Submitting to our spouses means first of all that we are
really glad they are exactly the way they are. If they are
difficult to live with, it is because we need that. There is no
better way to get rid of the rough edges of our own stubborn
ego. Aren't you glad for an opportunity to be changed into a
more loving, kind, and patient person?

True submission is a powerful thing. That is why Peter
wrote, "In like manner you married women, be submissive to
your own husbands . . . So that even if any do not obey the
Word of God, they may be won over *not by discussion* but by the
godly lives of their wives." (I Pet. 3:1 Amp)

Not long ago our office received the following note: "My
husband was an alcoholic for 35 years, and I was a self-
righteous goodie-two-shoes who probably drove him to it. Then
God showed me in the Bible that if I let Him put me in my right
place in the marriage, He would be responsible for my husband's place in His kingdom. I knelt by my husband's bed while
he was drunk, and asked him to forgive me for all the times I
had usurped his authority, and promised to be a submissive
wife from now on.

Guess what? God took charge immediately. My husband lay
in that bed for three days without moving. Then he got up and
has not been drunk since. He accepted Christ and His Holy
Spirit. Praise God! He is so wonderful."

There are wives who have lived for years under the domina-
tion of a demanding husband. They have learned an outward
adaption to keep peace in the house, but that is not a true
submission. If you are a suffering wife, examine your attitude.
Self-pity hides a complaint, and complaining is sin. Can you be
thankful your husband is the way he is? Or do you wish he
were different?

Submission isn't real until you *enjoy adapting yourself* to
your husband. When that happens, you will discover that God

has transformed you inside. You will know a greater joy and peace, and God's authority and power will be at work around you as well.

Marriage is a three-way relationship. Wife, whom do you think of as number one? It should be Jesus, with your husband a close second. If you think of yourself first, wanting attention, wanting to be loved more, you are not practicing love — because love does not seek self-satisfaction, but seeks to please the beloved.

Husband, whom do you think of as number one? It should be Jesus, with your wife a close second. A husband is placed in authority over his wife, but nowhere in the Bible is he told to enforce his authority. "And you husbands, show the same kind of love to your wives as Christ showed to the church when He died for her," (Eph. 5:25)

In many modern marriages husbands have left the decision making to their wives. If that is what you are doing, you are neglecting her true needs. God has appointed you as her head, to guide and direct her with the love of Christ, Who is your Head. If she doesn't want your advice — are you glad? That gives you an opportunity to depend on God and submit your wife to Him. If you let God put you in your right place as head of your wife, you can trust Him to be in charge of her submission as well. Your job is to concentrate on being glad she is the way she is, and to love her.

Wives and husbands have a way of bringing out the innermost rebellion in each other. That gives us wonderful opportunities again and again to see ourselves as we really are and to turn our sins over to God. We can't get rid of them as long as they remain hidden, so aren't you glad God gave you a wife or a husband who really knows how to get to you?

Perhaps the hardest thing to take from anybody is criticism. I was frequently hurt by people who found fault with me, and my natural reaction was to retaliate in kind. Then I began to understand that God allowed me to hear those words because

I needed them. If you are willing to *do* what God tells you to do, are you also willing to *hear* what He wants you to hear?

Jesus bore criticism and humiliation and never returned an ugly word. Sometimes what is said about us is true. David wrote, "Let the righteous smite me; it shall be a kindness: and let him reprove me; it shall be an excellent oil, which shall not break my head: . . ." (Ps. 141:5 KJV)

When someone finds fault with us, our first reaction should be to thank God. Be really glad. Then let the searchlight of the Holy Spirit show us if there is truth in the words. If there is, we need to confess.

If we are criticized unjustly, there is also reason to rejoice. This is a wonderful opportunity to demonstrate God's power in submission. If we answer in ugly words, the evil circle continues. If we respond in love, the circle is broken. The love of Christ takes the sting out of the words and brings promise of healing to the bitter and hurt soul of your accuser.

One day I was playing golf at Lawrence Welk's golf course with my friend, Roy Wyman. It was a beautiful day, and we walked leisurely on the green grass shaded by large trees. At the last hole we heard angry shouts behind us. A red-faced man shook his fist at us: "Don't you think of anyone but yourself?" he shouted, "There are people waiting to play after you!"

We had been so relaxed that we completely forgot to hurry with the game. For an instant I felt a flicker of the old Merlin, wanting to justify myself. Years ago I would have shaken my golf club and told the man to shut up! Instead, I felt a wave of compassion for the poor man, and was genuinely sorry that we had caused him pain. With a smile I apologized and watched as the purple color left his face. He muttered a word or two and left. Once his critical words would have ruined my afternoon. Now I felt peace and joy as I realized what a transformation God had brought in me.

Somehow we feel justified in not submitting to what we think is wrong. If our boss is critical of our religion, we feel we have "a right" to "stand up for Jesus" against company rules.

But what does the Bible say? "Servants, you must respect your masters and do whatever they tell you — not only if they are kind and reasonable, but even if they are tough and cruel." (I Pet. 2:18)

If your boss tells you to keep your mouth shut about Jesus during working hours — you should keep your mouth shut and be glad! Your boss couldn't talk to you like that unless you needed it. The most powerful Christian witness on the job is your joyful submission to whatever the boss asks of you. When you've learned what you need to learn, you'll be so glad your boss is the way he is that you don't care if he ever changes. You can praise God for him, and God's power and authority will radiate through that shop or office.

Is there a limit to your submission? Never in the inward attitude, but there may come a day when God says, "That's enough, now I want you to speak with my authority." If the boss says, "Go kill a man," you will have to say, "Sorry, Boss, can't do it." If he says, "Go get drunk!" you say, "Sorry Boss, can't do that either." But if he says, "Shut up and go back to work, you can say, "Yes, sir!"

The government may be wrong, but if we rebel against it, we are disobeying God. "Obey the government, for God is the one who has put it there. There is no government anywhere that God has not placed in power." (Rom. 13:1) That means communists or fascists or crooked officials. If you think the rules and regulations are getting too harsh; the taxes too high; the speed limit too low; they are that way because we need to learn submission. Are you grateful for the highway patrolman who stops you when you are speeding? Are you grateful for the IRS?

There may come a day when your government says, "Round up six million Jews and get rid of them!" That's when God will tell you to exercise His authority, and you can answer, "Sorry, government, I can't do that." Or they may say, "Deny your faith or you'll lose your freedom." And you say, "Sorry, government, you'll just have to put me in jail!" Or they may even

*Bringing Heaven into Hell*

kill you. That has happened to many Christians through the
years, and they counted it a joyous privilege to die for Christ.
Would you?

Most of us have a long way to go in the school of submission
before we get that far. We can't even submit to each other in
the church! All the different denominations are a result of
Christians not being able to submit to one another.

Why do you think God puts difficult people together in the
church? He does it so that we can learn to love each other. And
our love is not real until we can submit. Are there cantanker-
ous elders in your church? A stuffed-shirt pastor who tells
everybody what to do? A gossip in the pew? A sour Sunday
school teacher? Isn't the church as spiritual as you want it to
be? If you leave before His spirit leads you, you'll miss a
wonderful opportunity to learn submission. God can change
those people, and there is a good chance He will, when you've
learned to be really glad they are what they are.

Paul must have been a very proud man when he persecuted
the Christians before his own conversion. He was proud of his
superior education and wisdom; proud of his heritage and
position. It took many difficult and humiliating experiences to
teach Paul submission and true praise. But he learned. When
Paul spoke with authority, his inward submission was obvious.
He wrote, "Now . . . I have a command, not just a suggestion.
And it is not a command from me, for this is what the Lord
himself has said . . ." (I Cor. 7:10) Paul is saying, "I'm not
putting my own authority over you; it comes from God." Later
he wrote, "Here I want to add some suggestions of my own.
These are not direct commands from the Lord, but they seem
right to me! . . ." (I Cor. 7:12) He is careful not to command
when God had not given him specific authority.

When Paul wrote his letter to Philemon who was an elder
in the church at Colossae, he put aside his authority and
submitted to the other man. The letter concerns Philemon's
runaway slave, Onesimus, who became a Christian under
Paul's ministry in Rome. Paul sends him back to his master

with a letter: "... I could demand it of you in the name of
Christ because it is the right thing for you to do, but I love you
and prefer just to ask you . . . My plea is that you show
kindness to my child Onesimus, whom I won to the Lord . . . I
really wanted to keep him here . . . and you would have been
helping me through him, but I didn't want to do it without your
consent. I didn't want you to be kind because you had to but
because you wanted to." (Philemon, verses 8-10,13,14)

Paul had authority to demand obedience of Philemon, but
he knew that Philemon's submission would lose its power and
purpose unless it was voluntary. So Paul himself submits to
Philemon, saying that he will accept whatever the other man
chooses to do. He also gives Philemon the opportunity to do the
same to his slave, Onesimus, who voluntarily returns to submit
to his former master. Can you see how that kind of authority
and submission sets everybody free?

True authority never seeks to exalt itself or force others. It
seeks only the greatest good for those over whom it has been
placed. Jesus called himself a servant, and to demonstrate it
he knelt before his disciples and washed their feet. If you have
been placed in authority over someone at home, in church, at
work, in government, do you think of yourself as serving them?
Do you seek their greatest good, wanting their submission to
be mature and voluntary?

If there is conflict — are you glad? If someone is lazy,
careless, disrespectful, argumentative — are you grateful? Do
you know that God allows them to be like that to teach you true
authority? Do you think of Jesus as number one and your
difficult subordinate as a close number two? Can you see
yourself kneeling before him, washing his feet? If you can't,
there is something lacking in your submission, and your
authority isn't what God wants it to be. Are you glad you
discovered it? Now you can confess it and be forgiven and ask
God to remove any obstacle to true submission from your heart.

You can't separate authority from submission. Once you
really understand it, no one can take advantage of you and you

won't take advantage of others. You are learning to submit with joy to God's will whether He asks you to take authority or to be a doormat. If He wants you to be a doormat, be the happiest doormat ever, because you are learning to be what God wants you to be, and your praise will flow from a heart filled with the joy of Christ. Jesus said, ". . . Well done, thou good and faithful servant: . . . enter thou into the joy of thy lord." (Matt. 25:21 KJV) You are seeing Heaven flow into Hell.

## 11. In Love With God

My grandmother was one of the happiest people I ever knew. When she was dying, both of her legs had turned black with gangrene, making even the room stink. People came to sympathize, but left filled with astonishment at the joy coming from Grandmother's lips. The only thing she could think of was that she would soon be with her beloved Jesus. From a human standpoint, Grandmother's circumstances were horrible, but for years her attention had been so focused on Christ that joy was the theme of her life.

My father was like her. He worked in a steel mill in Pennsylvania as a laborer. When I was a young man, seven years after my Father's death, I got a job in the same mill. I had a small office near the steel furnaces where Dad had worked. An elderly Roman Catholic Italian worker often came to see me, always removing his hat before speaking, "If you ever become a Christian, Merlin, become a Christian like your father."

"What do you mean?" I felt awkward.

"Your father was always happy. He went along the steel furnaces and when he found someone who was tired or discouraged he talked to him, then stepped off to the side. We could see him raise his hands and knew he was thanking God."

The stories always embarrassed me, just as I had been embarrassed as a boy when I sat on the front row in church

with my father. He would sometimes explode with joy in that
staid Methodist church, jump to his feet and say, "Praise the
Lord!" I wanted to hide under my seat, but Mother was proud of
him, for she had prayed for many years that Jesus would
become real to him.

Dad was only thirty-six years old when he died, but I
remember the happiness that was so typical of his life, as he sat
up in bed and said, "Look, they are here to take me!" Then he
leaned back against his pillow and was gone.

It took many years before I began to understand the secret
of grandmother's and father's happiness. They were certain of
God's love. They knew Him and trusted Him and saw every
circumstance as a gift from His hand — even pain and death.

It has long been the desire of my heart to be able to praise
God like that. One day recently I was thinking about it, and
felt a nudge inside: "Come up higher, Merlin." The thought
was repeated several times, and I wondered what it meant. All
I could think of was high mountains and airplanes. Perhaps I
needed to do more hiking and flying!

A small squirrel ran straight up a tree in front of me, and
my heart gave an involuntary leap. What if the squirrel caught
hold of a piece of loose bark and tumbled to his death? As I
watched, he ran even higher, to the very top of the tree, and out
on a tiny limb that bent and swayed under his weight. It was
fearful just to watch, but as the squirrel moved gracefully back
and forth high up against the blue sky, I suddenly perceived
that he was having a wonderful time. What seemed like a
dangerous height to me was his natural environment. He was
more at home in the tree tops than on the ground.

I felt that little nudge again: "Come up higher, Merlin, up
here with Me where you belong. You'll have a wonderful time!"
We human beings are as frightened of spiritual heights as we
are of physical heights. We don't want to fall, and so we think
we are safer on the ground, even if we belong up higher. God
says, "I created you for fellowship with me. I want you up here
in the clean and pure air of Christian maturity, not down

where the pollution of filth and degradation will discourage and pull you down."

"Lord," I thought. "I want to come up higher, but how do I get there?"

My mind went to the story of Jesus meeting the woman at the well in Samaria. He told her that the water in the well could only quench her thirst for a little while, but He had water to give that would become like a well springing up inside her, flowing continuously with eternal life. The woman said she would like some of that water, and then she asked a question that seemed unrelated to the topic: "Where are we supposed to worship God; on a mountain in Samaria, or in Jerusalem?"

Jesus answered her, "You (Samaritans) do not know what you are worshipping — you worship what you do not comprehend . . . A time will come, however, indeed it is already here, when the true (genuine) worshippers will worship the Father in spirit and in truth (reality); for the Father is seeking just such people as these as His worshippers." (Jn. 4:22,23 Amp)

"But, Lord," I thought. "I already know about that well of living water — it is the Holy Spirit inside me — and I know something about worshipping you in Spirit and in Truth . . ."

"To worship in Spirit and in Truth is a continuous thing, like the well of living water never running dry — are you doing that?"

"No, Lord . . ."

"Do you want to come up higher?"

"Yes, Lord . . ." There was a long silence, and I thought how often we come to church, sit down, sing songs, say, "Praise the Lord," and we are not worshipping in Spirit and in Truth. As we begin to learn to praise Him, we see answered prayers, and our praise makes us feel good and satisfied for a time — then discouragement sets in and we are thirsty again.

The question formed itself in my mind, "What makes the well inside me flow continuously?"

"The more you love Me, the more it flows . . ."

"But I do love You . . ."

There was silence, and my eyes fell on the words in my Bible: "You worship what you do not comprehend." The meaning was suddenly clear. When our worship is empty, it is because we don't understand or comprehend enough about God, and we can't love what we don't know. Often I have heard people say, "How can I really love God? I don't see Him, I know He is almighty and great — how can a small human being actually love something that big and vague?"

Most of us will have to admit that to love God is a difficult concept at times, but then to love Him is not something that we human beings can do on our own. "We love him, because he first loved us." (I John 4:19 KJV) It is when God's love reaches us that we can respond by loving Him. Once we have accepted the love He offers us through Christ, we are told by Jesus Himself, ". . . Thou shalt love the Lord thy God with all thy heart, and with all thy soul, and with all thy mind. This is the first and great commandment." (Matt. 22:37,38 KJV)

So loving God is not just something desirable for us to do; it is a command. We must come to God and say, "How do I learn to love you?" Jesus tells us how to proceed: ". . . If a man love me, He will keep my word;. . ." (John 14:23 KJV)

Love is a verb, an action word, and we love God by doing what He tells us to do. When He says, "Express your love in praising Me for everything," we start doing it because He says we should, whether we feel like it or not.

The more we obey Him, the better we get to know Him, and the more we will want to love Him and obey Him some more. Jesus said, "The one who obeys Me is the one who loves Me; and because he loves Me, my Father will love him; and I will too, and I will reveal myself to him." (Jn 14:21)

Where do you think Jesus will reveal Himself? — in the very circumstances where before we could see only suffering.

Sandra, a young housewife in her late twenties, had suffered with terrible migraine headaches since she was a teenager. The headaches would come without warning, virtually crippling her for the 24 to 48 hours they lasted. Her vision would blur, she would have a fever, and no medical or therapeutical remedies seemed to help.

When she became a Christian, she cried to God for relief, but the pain did not diminish. At times she thought that since she was now assured eternal life with Christ, she would be better off dead than suffering such agony.

One day she was given my book *Walking and Leaping*. The idea of thanking God for everything was new to her, and she wasn't sure she agreed with it. A few days later she was at a party when the headache struck again. She confided in a friend and explained that she would have to hurry home before her vision blurred so that she could no longer drive.

"Have you ever thought of thanking God for your headaches?"

"Of course not!" Sandra was visibly shaken. "I thank Him for good things, but how can I blame Him for something as horrible as this pain? It would not be right."

"Then do you mind if I thank Him for you?" the friend asked. "You see, I believe God is more powerful than your pain, and He could take it away if He wanted. Since He hasn't taken it away, doesn't it make sense that He must want you to have it for a good reason? So why not thank Him for it and see what happens?"

Sandra listened as her friend quoted several scriptures emphasizing that we should thank God for all things. Then she nodded resolutely. "I know God is more powerful than my pain," she said. "I've always wondered why He allowed me to have these headaches. But if He says I should thank Him, then I promise to try it — even if it kills me." She grimaced and her face showed the increasing pain. "God must know better than I do what's good for me, and I want to obey Him . . ."

During the next 24 hours Sandra made an important discovery. When she directed her thoughts to God and thanked Him for her agony, it became more bearable. When she let her attention focus on the pain itself, it became worse. "So You *are* in control of my pain, aren't You, God?" she whispered into the darkness of the night. "I thank You for showing me that You are really here and care about my headache."

That night, for the first time since the headaches had begun, she did not get out of bed to try to find a remedy for her pain. She did not apply ice packs or take cold showers or swallow any pain pills. Instead, she told God, "Now that I know you are in control, I know You know best what I can take. You won't make it harder than I can bear. Thank You."

The next morning her husband saw her fever blisters and said, "Honey, you must have had a bad night. Why didn't you wake me as usual?"

"It was bad, but it was all right," she smiled. "God was there, and He was in charge of my pain. I know I can take anything He gives me."

Several weeks later some member of Sandra's family came to our church and asked special prayer for her. They felt assured that God heard and healed her, and returned home with the good news to a surprised Sandra, "You will never have another of those pains."

Two weeks later the headache struck again, as blinding as ever, but Sandra confided happily to her friend, "So God didn't want me to get healed yet, but I actually consider myself lucky to have those pains. God is using them to show me how much He loves me. My husband was disappointed that I didn't get healed, but I told him, 'Don't worry, Just let me lie still and enjoy what God wants to teach me this time.'" Her voice bubbled with happiness. "I am getting to know God in a completely new way. All those hours when I have the pain, God is right there with me. I talk to Him like I never do when I'm running around with my daily activities. I am quiet, and His presence becomes so real. He makes me feel very loved and very special."

Sandra's voice faltered, "To think of the years I spent feeling sorry for myself. Why, the very thing I complained about has turned out to be one of the biggest blessings of my life."

She had prayed that her mother would find a personal relationship with Jesus, and said, "Since I started thanking God for my pain, Mother has become very curious about Christianity. She watched me all those years nearly going out of my mind with the headaches. Now she sees that something real has happened to me. Wouldn't it be wonderful if God could use my pains to show Mother His love?"

Sandra believes that God may take her pains away some day. "But He won't do it as long as He has something wonderful to teach me through them, and I'm glad!"

Sandra discovered what Paul meant when he wrote, "Therefore, I take pleasure in infirmities, in reproaches, in necessities, in persecutions, in distresses for Christ's sake: for when I am weak, then am I strong." (II Cor. 12:10 KJV)

Paul took pleasure in problems and pain. He didn't endure them, he enjoyed them. You may not understand why your problems or your pain are there, but of one thing you may be sure — if you enjoy them, they will reveal to you the hidden treasures of God's love.

I was in Alaska when someone pointed out a hill where a man named Ed Lung sat, broke and discouraged, during the Gold Rush Days of 1897. Ed was one of the first to arrive in Alaska when gold was discovered, but somehow he was always a day late to any site where gold was found. One day he sat on a hill, nearly weeping, and decided he might as well go back home to Tacoma, Washington, empty-handed and broke. A few weeks later another man put a pick into that same spot and discovered the famous Gold Hill that produced a billion dollars worth of the precious metal.

Are you sitting discouraged and dejected over the very problem that may be the source of your greatest joy if you will obey God and thank Him for it?

God wants you to trust Him and love Him enough to obey Him. Have you ever been to dinner at someone's house and they served something you had never before seen? You didn't know whether you should take a small spoonful just to be polite, or fill your plate. Your wife, sitting next to you, whispered, "Honey, I know what it is — you will love it!" Without hesitation you would take a big serving, because you know that your wife knows exactly what you like best.

If you can trust your wife like that, can't you trust God when certain circumstances come into your life, and He leans over to whisper, "I know what that is — you love it!"

To reject what God gives us is to disobey Him, and it means we don't love Him. To say we love Him when we disobey Him is a contradiction. It doesn't work. Jesus said, "If ye keep my commandments, ye shall abide in my love;. . ." (Jn. 15:10 KJV)

If you've been disobedient, you need to confess it and say, "Lord, I'm sorry I don't care enough about you to do what you want. Please forgive me and help me to love you more."

When you tell God that, you are saying that you want to come up higher, and He only asks two things of you: That you show your love by obeying Him to the best of your ability — and that you declare your love for Him in worship and praise.

Why does God need people to tell Him how great He is? He doesn't need it, but we need to do it. God knows His greatness, but we are still learning about it. When we praise Him for all He has done for us, it does something inside us and we see more of His greatness than we did before. The Holy Spirit within us joins in our praises, and we are lifted up higher and higher.

Tell God daily that you want to love Him more, and confess when you find yourself complaining. We can't love God enough as long as we're living in our old bodies, but God rejoices to see us do the best we can. That is all He asks, and He loves us just as we are. Try making a list of all the reasons you have to love God. You'll find it growing day by day. Thank Him for each item. Say it loud; sing about your blessings. Share them with others.

Paul advised the Christians in Ephesus: "Talk with each other much about the Lord, quoting psalms and hymns and

singing sacred songs, making music in your hearts to the
Lord." (Eph. 5:19) As you make it your regular practice, you
will find yourself lifted high above your depressions and
moods, and your love of God will grow and grow.

A young woman named Gloria complained a great deal
about her housework, and her husband accused her of being
sloppy and careless. It was true that her house never looked
very neat. One day she heard about praising God for everything, and realized that her complaining was a serious sin. She
told God she was sorry and promised to do her best to be
obedient in the future. She began by thanking Him for the
things she disliked the most; the greasy stove top, the cluttered
refrigerator, the dirty floors. As she went about the house, she
suddenly realized that God had given her all those things. He
would not give her anything unless it was very special and
precious, and He wanted her to love the very things she had
never liked.

It was an exciting discovery for Gloria. "I began to see that
God loved my house and my things. Each chair, each rug, each
picture, each pot, and each dish suddenly looked different. How
I had neglected them before! I asked God to forgive me for not
loving the things He had given me enough to take care of them.
Whenever I found a neglected corner, I said, 'You poor corner.
God loves you and I love you, and I won't neglect you any
more.' " She laughed as she shared her story. "I'm falling in
love with my house, and I even love me! I hated my own
carelessness and sloppiness, but God forgives every mistake I
make, and all He asks is that I do my best. He only wants me to
love Him as much as I can, and each day I love Him a little
more."

Housework was no longer dull. Gloria's brown eyes shone
with excitement. "This new love of mine is more solid than an
emotion. It isn't affected by how I feel from one day to the next.
When I think of how God loves me, I just *have* to love
everything He gives me. I even love the dirty footprints my
children leave on the living room rug and the greasy smears

from their hands on the walls. I say, 'Thank You, Lord, for those dirt marks. Thank You for my children, help me to love them even more.' And I feel the love swell inside me, and I am the luckiest person in the world with so much to love."

Her husband no longer complains about a messy house. The rooms are neat, flowers bloom in pots and Gloria's kitchen usually smells of good cooking. She has discovered what Paul meant when he talked about taking pleasure in necessities. So often it is the little things we *have* to do — like getting up in the morning, doing dishes, washing the car, shopping for groceries or patching a hole in the roof — that gets us to complain. But God assigned each of our chores with special care, and we are told, "And whatever work you may have to do, do everything in the name of the Lord Jesus, thanking God the Father through Him." (Col. 3:17 Phillips) Each of the things we *have* to do should be a declaration of love to God — and His love will lift us even higher.

Is there someone you really adore? Perhaps your wife or your husband, or your first grandchild? Just looking at them makes you want to melt. You love to be near them. You praise them continuously, and you think of things to do to make them happy. You love them, not for what they do for you, but for what they are. This is the kind of relationship God has given my wife, Mary, and me. We have never had an argument, a cross word, or even the slightest desire that the other person would change in any way. We marvel continually that God would choose to give us such perfect, undeserved, unending harmony.

She does give me one problem, however. She occasionally wakes me during the night with her gentle laughter. She is asleep, murmuring, "Thank You, Jesus," and then another soft, happy laugh. Her happiness does also give us another minor problem. After Mary had given her testimony during one of our city-wide crusades, I asked the audience who had been thinking, "She surely is a lot younger than Merlin." About ninety percent of the audience raised their hands. I told

If this book has been a blessing to you, please let me know. Fill out this card and drop it in the mail. Thank you! I'll send you a free copy of our monthly Praise News so you can continue learning about the benefits of praising the Lord.

**Merlin R. Carothers**

*(Please Print)*

NAME _____

ADDRESS _____

CITY _____ STATE _____ ZIP _____

**FOUNDATION OF PRAISE**
**P.O. Box 2518**
**Escondido, CA 92025**

them I knew the Lord would forgive them and shared that she
is the mother of a twenty-four year old boy. The Oh's and Ah's
showed they could hardly believe she was more than twenty-
four years old herself. Happiness and love make some people
look many years younger than they are.

When our love for God reaches a certain point, we begin to
adore Him. Our hearts overflow with unspeakable praise, and
we say, "Father, I don't want you to do anything for me. I just
want to be near you and love you. I don't need another blessing
to quench my spiritual thirst. I am satisfied because you love
me, Lord, and I love everything you give me."

David wrote, "Bless — affectionately, gratefully praise —
the Lord, O my soul, and all that is (deepest) within me, bless
His holy name!" (Ps. 103:1 Amp) When all that is deepest
within us affectionately and gratefully says, "God, I really love
you!", the well within begins to flow uninterrupted. Your
Christian life doesn't go up and down any more, it just goes
higher. You don't need to ask anyone to pray that you will feel
good, because the well inside keeps flowing.

Your joy doesn't come through being healed, wonderful as
that may be. It doesn't come through having your prayers
answered, wonderful as that may be. It comes from being in
love with God.

One of the most joyful people I have ever met came to our
church on a bed. Esther Lee was blind, paralyzed, and could
only move her thumb on one hand. Her bones were so brittle
that they would break if her limbs were moved.

When I spoke to her over the phone earlier, her voice rang
with confident happiness, like someone abundantly blessed
with every good thing. I knew she had been in bed for many
years with rheumatoid arthritis. Not long ago her doctors had
given her up and told her husband to prepare her for heaven. A
friend had brought *Prison to Praise* and read it out loud to her
three times. With nothing to lose, she had determined to try
praising God for her pain instead of blaming Him. It became
the turning point in her life.

She kept up the praise while calamities befell her household; a bankrupt business, her husband's heart attack, the children's sicknesses. Through it all she began to glimpse the love of God in a new way. "He showed me what a snivelling, miserable, complaining and bitter creature I had been all my life, and as I cried for forgiveness, His love came down to heal my sin-sick soul and fill me with joy and peace."

Her voice was weakened by her condition, but she kept exclaiming out loud, "God, I praise you, God, I love you," until her voice grew stronger. She had never had an ear for music, but as she praised God, melodies and words came to her mind. She began to sing, and her voice developed a quality it had never had before. Others were blessed by her singing and persuaded her to make a recording, named "Where Glory Began."

A phone was installed by her bed. It could be operated by her one thumb, so that she could talk to people from all over the United States who began calling her to be encouraged in *their faith!*

To come to our church, she traveled all the way from her home in Palm Springs to Escondido in a U-Haul trailer wide enough to carry her bed. The day was hot and the closed-in trailer felt like a tin oven. The trip had to have been torturing. Esther Lee had waited two years for an opportunity to visit us, and believed that she would be healed the minute she entered the church.

What happened instead made a greater impression on those present, I believe, than if she had leaped from her bed. She thanked God in such heartfelt praise that we knew she was rejoicing. Lying on her bed at the front of the church, she spoke to the congregation for the next hour of the blessings God had given her. She led in singing and praising with a voice bubbling with laughter.

Her physical condition was such that those who saw her would be tempted to feel pity and sorrow. Instead, we were moved to laughter and tears as we glimpsed, beyond the weak and wasted body on the bed, a beautiful relationship with God. She was blind and immobile, yet she was teaching us about the glorious power in praise. She spoke of finding life in surrender, and finding the amazing, intimate love of God through pain and sufferings more severe than most of us could imagine.

Love shone in her face as she led us in singing praises to our Heavenly Father — a love not dependent on what He does for us, but on what He has already done in Christ. It was a love stronger than the greatest physical infirmity — a love that sees God through blind eyes. I thought of David's Psalm: "Let the saints be joyful in glory; let them sing aloud upon their beds." (Ps. 149:5 KJV)

Are you singing praises to God? In pain, in problems, in difficult circumstances, can you sing aloud, "I love You, God; I thank You, God; I praise You, God!"

Or are you discouraged, waiting for God to come from somewhere outside to comfort you? Listen and you will hear him say, "Come up a little higher, learn to love me . . ." If you don't love Him enough, love Him as much as you can. You love Him a little, don't you? He forgives you for not loving Him more, and He will help you as you begin saying, "I love You as much as I can, Lord, help me to love You more."

Paul wrote, "And the Lord direct your hearts into the love of God; . . ." (II Thess. 3:5 KJV) Jesus Himself will direct our hearts when we sincerely desire to love God. As you obey His directions, you will discover a comfort that doesn't come from a change in your outward circumstances. Something happens inside you when you begin to love God more. A well of living water starts flowing continuously, until you worship God in Spirit and in Truth. Your problems are designed to help you do it. When that well flows within you, it no longer matters whether your problems stay with you or go away. What matters is that you are in love with God.

It is that love Paul speaks of "The ultimate aim of the Christian ministry, after all, is to produce the love which springs from a pure heart, a good conscience and a genuine

faith." (I Tim. 1:5 Phillips) When you love like that, you will
praise God till the day you die. During the last day of his life,
Charles Wesley was heard whispering the words of the hymn,
"I'll praise my Maker while I live." As he grew weaker, he
could only say, "I'll praise, I'll praise." He repeated the words
till his last breath was gone.

The Bible is full of passages reminding us of the greatness
of our Heavenly Father. Reading them aloud helps us express
our love for Him. One of my favorites is Psalm 103. It gives me
wonderful reason to say, "God, I really love You!"

> "Bless — affectionately, gratefully praise — the Lord, O my
>     soul,
> and all that is (deepest) within me, bless His holy name!
> He ransoms me from Hell.
> He surrounds me with lovingkindness and tender mercies.
> He fills my life with good things!
> My youth is renewed like the eagle's!
> He gives justice to all who are treated unfairly.
> He revealed His will and nature to Moses and the people of
>     Israel.
> He is merciful and tender toward those who don't deserve it;
> He is slow to get angry and full of kindness and love.
> He never bears a grudge, nor remains angry forever.
> He has not punished us as we deserve for all our sins,
>     for His mercy toward those who fear and honor
>     Him is as great as the height of the heavens above
>     the earth.
> He has removed our sins as far away from us as the east is
>     from the west.                            (Amp and Living)
>
> *He has brought His Heaven into what was once*
>     *my Hell.*

If this book has been a blessing to you, please let me know. Each month I prepare **Praise News** in which I share new things that I learn about praise. I will be pleased to send this to you at no charge if you request it. Write to:

**Merlin R. Carothers**
**Box 1430**
**Escondido, CA 92025**

Merlin Carothers traces the practical uses of praise in all of his books — the simple application of Biblical truth: **all things work together for good ... in everything give thanks ... count it all joy.**

---

## PRISON TO PRAISE
Merlin Carothers first book. This book has been printed in thirty-one languages and distributed in over sixty countries. Many people have reported transformed lives as a result of reading the powerful message found in this book.

## PRISON TO PRAISE — Large Print

## POWER IN PRAISE
An in-depth study of the working and scriptural basis for the principle introduced in *Prison to Praise:* in all things give praise and thanks to God. Praising God in one's predicaments is first acknowledging that God is in control of everything, whether or not it is in His will, and that He has the power to turn all things to good. Secondly, the act of obediently praising God begins to soften our hearts and produces a right heart attitude — a prerequisite for any act of God.

## ANSWERS TO PRAISE
The proof of the pudding! No sooner did the first two Praise books come out than the phone calls and letters started pouring in. Praise works! Overjoyed Christians felt compelled to share the "signs and wonders following" with the author, adding their own testimonies to the rapidly-growing record. Miracle upon miracle, from all walks of life!

## PRAISE WORKS
More letters selected from an assortment of thousands illustrate the secret of *freedom through praise!* Includes a letter from Frank Foglio — (author of *Hey, God!*) — who learned the power of praise when his daughter recovered miraculously after 7 long years in the "hopeless" ward of an institution for the mentally ill. Other letters are from a nurse, a nun, an attorney, a blind girl, a chaplain, an alcoholic and many others! Praise for brain surgery, praise for prison, praise for the Lord!

## WALKING AND LEAPING

When Merlin Carothers lost a new car and trailer, along with his most-prized possessions, in a freak traffic accident — he praised God. But when he found himself singlehandedly overseeing the construction of a massive church building with only the enthusiastic but unskilled labor of his parishioners, and with the precarious backing of a bank balance that generally registered zero, he had to learn to "praise God in all things" all over again. "Fascinating and exciting. I thoroughly enjoyed it."
— New Life Magazine

## VICTORY ON PRAISE MOUNTAIN

When Merlin Carothers met with contention and dissension in his church, he learned to apply in his own life the principles he has taught to millions of others. This intensely personal account shows how genuine, spontaneous praise often leads into valleys that are direct paths to higher ground.

## THE BIBLE ON PRAISE

This beautifully-printed, four-color, thirty-two page booklet features selected verses on praise from thirty-eight books of the Bible. These are Merlin's favorite verses and were personally selected by him. This booklet makes a lovely gift with a message that will bless the reader for years.

## MORE POWER TO YOU

Worldwide demand for more information on power has resulted in *More Power To You* — written for persons in everyday places who need more power in their everyday lives. Though presented in simple easy-to-read language, the author had given us profound and useful insights into serious problems of modern life. This book is a beautiful key to unlock a vast storehouse of spiritual power.

Comments, inquiries and requests for speaking engagements should be directed to

Merlin R. Carothers
Box 1430
Escondido, California 92025

The following recorded messages by Merlin R. Carothers are available through the Merlin R. Carothers Company:

Special prepared album of six messages in unusually attractive case, titles are:

## Volume I

1. *How God Taught Me to Praise*
2. *Start Trusting*
3. *Real Faith*
4. *Set Free*
5. *Taming the Tongue*
6. *Leap for Joy*

## Volume II

1. *No Fear in Love*
2. *Christian Love*
3. *Recreated Faith*
4. *Seek Ye First*
5. *Lost Battles*
6. *Created to Believe*

available at $23.95 for either album.

The Merlin R. Carothers Company
Box 1430
Escondido, CA 92025